JOURNEYING WITH GOD

INTERNATIONAL THEOLOGICAL COMMENTARY

Fredrick Carlson Holmgren and George A. F. Knight
General Editors

Volumes now available

Genesis 1–11: From Eden to Babel
by Donald E. Gowan

Genesis 12–50: Abraham and All the Families of the Earth
by J. Gerald Janzen

Numbers: Journeying with God
by Katharine Doob Sakenfeld

Deuteronomy: Word and Presence
by Ian Cairns

Joshua: Inheriting the Land
by E. John Hamlin

Judges: At Risk in the Promised Land
by E. John Hamlin

1 and 2 Samuel: Let Us Be like the Nations
by Gnana Robinson

1 Kings: Nations under God
by Gene Rice

Ezra and Nehemiah: Israel Alive Again
by Fredrick Carlson Holmgren

Proverbs and Ecclesiastes: Who Knows What Is Good?
by Kathleen A. Farmer

Song of Songs and Jonah: Revelation of God
by George A. F. Knight
and Friedemann W. Golka

Isaiah 1–39: The Lord Is Savior: Faith in National Crisis
by S. H. Widyapranawa

Isaiah 40–55: Servant Theology
by George A. F. Knight

Isaiah 56–66: The New Israel
by George A. F. Knight

Jeremiah 1–25: To Pluck Up, To Tear Down
by Walter Brueggemann

Jeremiah 26–52: To Build, To Plant
by Walter Brueggemann

Ezekiel: A New Heart
by Bruce Vawter and Leslie J. Hoppe

Daniel: Signs and Wonders
by Robert A. Anderson

Hosea: Grace Abounding
by H. D. Beeby

Joel and Malachi: A Promise of Hope, A Call to Obedience
by Graham S. Ogden
and Richard R. Deutsch

Amos and Lamentations: God's People in Crisis
by Robert Martin-Achard
and S. Paul Re'emi

Micah: Justice and Loyalty
by Juan I. Alfaro

Nahum, Obadiah, and Esther: Israel among the Nations
by Richard J. Coggins
and S. Paul Re'emi

Habakkuk and Zephaniah: Wrath and Mercy
by Mária Eszenyei Széles

Haggai and Zechariah: Rebuilding with Hope
by Carroll Stuhlmueller, C.P.

Forthcoming

Ruth: Surely There Is a Future
by E. John Hamlin

JOURNEYING WITH GOD

A Commentary on the Book of

Numbers

KATHARINE DOOB SAKENFELD

WM. B. EERDMANS PUBLISHING CO., GRAND RAPIDS

THE HANDSEL PRESS LTD, EDINBURGH

© 1995 Wm. B. Eerdmans Publishing Company
First published 1995 by Wm. B. Eerdmans Publishing Company,
255 Jefferson Ave. S.E., Grand Rapids, Michigan 49503
and
The Handsel Press Limited
The Stables, Carberry, EH21 8PY, Scotland

00 99 98 97 96 95   7 6 5 4 3 2 1

Library of Congress Cataloging-in-Publication Data

Sakenfeld, Katharine Doob, 1940-
Journeying with God: a commentary on the book of Numbers /
Katharine Doob Sakenfeld.
p.   cm. — (International theological commentary)
Includes bibliographical references (p.).
ISBN 0-8028-4126-0 (alk. paper)
1. Bible. O.T. Numbers — Commentaries. I. Title. II. Series.
BS1265.3.S25 1995
222'.1407 — dc20   95-24163
                                                      CIP

Handsel Press ISBN 1 871828 25 2

CONTENTS

JOURNEYING WITH GOD

CONTENTS

ABBREVIATIONS

NJPS   New Jewish Publication Society version
NRSV   New Revised Standard Version
REB   Revised English Bible
RSV   Revised Standard Version
SBL   Society of Biblical Literature

EDITORS' PREFACE

The Old Testament alive in the Church: this is the goal of the *International Theological Commentary*. Arising out of changing, unsettled times, this Scripture speaks with an authentic voice to our own troubled world. It witnesses to God's ongoing purpose and to God's caring presence in the universe without ignoring those experiences of life that cause one to question God's existence and love. This commentary series is written by front-rank scholars who treasure the life of faith.

Addressed to ministers and Christian educators, the *International Theological Commentary* moves beyond the usual critical-historical approach to the Bible and offers a *theological* interpretation of the Hebrew text. Thus, engaging larger textual units of the biblical writings, the authors of these volumes assist the reader in the appreciation of the theology underlying the text as well as its place in the thought of the Hebrew Scriptures. But more, since the Bible is the book of the believing community, its text has acquired ever more meaning through an ongoing interpretation. This growth of interpretation may be found both within the Bible itself and in the continuing scholarship of the Church.

Contributors to the *International Theological Commentary* are Christians — persons who affirm the witness of the New Testament concerning Jesus Christ. For Christians, the Bible is *one* Scripture containing the Old and New Testaments. For this reason, a commentary on the Old Testament may not ignore the second part of the canon, namely, the New Testament.

Since its beginning, the Church has recognized a special relationship between the two Testaments. But the precise character of this bond has been difficult to define. Thousands of books and articles have discussed the issue. The diversity of views represented in these publications makes us aware that the Church is not of one mind in expressing the "how" of this relationship. The authors of this commentary share a developing consensus that any serious explanation of the Old Testament's relationship to the New will uphold the integrity of the Old Testament. Even though Christianity is rooted in the soil of the Hebrew Scriptures, the biblical interpreter must take care lest he or she "christianize" these Scriptures.

Authors writing in this commentary will, no doubt, hold varied views concerning *how* the Old Testament relates to the New. No attempt has been made to dictate one viewpoint in this matter. With the whole Church, we are convinced that the relationship between the two Testaments is real and substantial. But we recognize also the diversity of opinions among Christian scholars when they attempt to articulate fully the nature of this relationship.

In addition to the Christian Church, there exists another people for whom the Old Testament is important, namely, the Jewish community. Both Jews and Christians claim the Hebrew Bible as Scripture. Jews believe that the basic teachings of this Scripture point toward, and are developed by, the Talmud, which assumed its present form about 500 C.E. On the other hand, Christians hold that the Old Testament finds its fulfillment in the New Testament. The Hebrew Bible, therefore, belongs to both the Church and the Synagogue.

Recent studies have demonstrated how profoundly early Christianity reflects a Jewish character. This fact is not surprising because the Christian movement arose out of the context of first-century Judaism. Further, Jesus himself was Jewish, as were the first Christians. It is to be expected, therefore, that Jewish and Christian interpretations of the Hebrew Bible will reveal similarities *and* disparities. Such is the case. The authors of the *International Theological Commentary* will refer to the various Jewish traditions that they consider important for an appreciation of the Old Testament text. Such references will enrich our understanding of certain biblical passages and, as an extra gift, offer us insight into the relationship of Judaism to early Christianity.

An important second aspect of the present series is its *international* character. In the past, Western church leaders were considered to be *the* leaders of the Church — at least by those living in the West! The theology and biblical exegesis done by these scholars dominated the thinking of the Church. Most commentaries were produced in the Western world and reflected the lifestyle, needs, and thoughts of its civilization. But the Christian Church is a worldwide community. People who belong to this universal Church reflect differing thoughts, needs, and lifestyles.

Today the fastest growing churches in the world are to be found, not in the West, but in Africa, Indonesia, South America, Korea, Taiwan, and elsewhere. By the end of this century, Christians in these areas will outnumber those who live in the West. In our age, especially, a commentary on the Bible must transcend the parochialism of Western civilization and be sensitive to issues that are the special problems of persons who live outside of the "Christian" West, issues such as race relations, personal survival and fulfillment, liberation, revolution, famine, tyranny, disease, war, the poor, and religion and state. Inspired of God, the authors of the Old Testament knew what life is like on the edge of existence. They addressed themselves to everyday people who often faced more than everyday problems. Refusing to limit God to the "spiritual," they portrayed God as one who heard and knew the cries of people in pain (see Exod. 3:7-8). The contributors to the *International Theological Commentary* are persons who prize the writings of these biblical authors as a word of life to our world today. They read the Hebrew Scriptures in the twin contexts of ancient Israel and our modern day.

The scholars selected as contributors underscore the international aspect of the series. Representing very different geographical, ideological, and ecclesiastical backgrounds, they come from more than seventeen countries. Besides scholars from such traditional countries as England, Scotland, France, Italy, Switzerland, Canada, New Zealand, Australia, South Africa, and the United States, contributors from the following places are included: Israel, Indonesia, India, Thailand, Singapore, Taiwan, and countries of Eastern Europe. Such diversity makes for richness of thought. Christian scholars living in Buddhist, Muslim, or Socialist lands may be able to offer the World Church insights into the biblical message — insights to which the scholarship of the West could be blind.

The proclamation of the biblical message is the focal concern of the *International Theological Commentary*. Generally speaking, the authors of these commentaries value the historical-critical studies of past scholars, but they are convinced that these studies by themselves are not enough. The Bible is more than an object of critical study; it is the revelation of God. In the written Word, God has disclosed himself and his will to humankind. Our authors see themselves as servants of the Word which, when rightly received, brings *shalom* to both the individual and the community.

GEORGE A. F. KNIGHT
FREDRICK CARLSON HOLMGREN

AUTHOR'S PREFACE

Insofar as I am able, I have written this commentary for the church in its diversity of race, gender, geographic and social location, and theological perspective; at the same time, I have written the commentary for the church in its unity in commitment to Jesus Christ and to the gospel to which the entire Bible, Old and New Testament alike, bears witness. In dealing with the book of Numbers, relatively unknown to most Christians, I have attempted to comment on points that would be obscure or confusing to general readers, as well as to suggest the ongoing importance of the material for aspects of Christian life. On many points where scholarship is divided or speculative, I have simply noted the uncertainty of our knowledge.

It is my view, in common with the preponderance of contemporary Western scholarship, that most of the book of Numbers reflects concerns of Israelites/Jews living hundreds of years after the wilderness era that the text purports to describe, and that the book was compiled over time rather than being composed by a single author. Nonetheless, I have chosen to focus mainly on the received form of the text, rather than on its component parts, and I have not tried to argue the questions of dating or of historicity. It is my hope that the commentary can be read profitably for theological reflection even by those whose presuppositions about the history of Israel and the history of composition of the text differ widely from my own.

I thank Fredrick Holmgren, George A. F. Knight, and Allen Myers for their patience and support during the work on this project. The Trustees of Princeton Theological Seminary graciously granted me sabbatical time to work on the commentary.

The help of Carolyn Pressler, Linda Day, and Morag Logan with research and copyediting was invaluable. I extend a special word of appreciation to the many pastors who have engaged with me in reflection on the book of Numbers in continuing education settings over the past years; their insights and encouragement have contributed more than they can know.

This book is dedicated with gratitude and affection to my husband Helmar, whose laughter brings sunshine to our life's journey with God.

KATHARINE DOOB SAKENFELD
Eastertide 1994

INTRODUCTION

How faithful is God to promises made to an ungrateful and rebellious people? Does God give people a second chance? What does it mean to be a holy community, and how is that sanctity to be maintained? What kind of leadership does a journeying people need on its way between promise and fulfillment? How does God provide when the leaders struggle under their burden or even abandon their task? These are some of the important questions addressed in the book of Numbers.

The book of Numbers is the fourth of the five books in the Pentateuch or Torah, the first major division of the Hebrew Bible. The book opens with the people of Israel encamped at the foot of Mt. Sinai, receiving instructions from God through the word of their leader, Moses. At the conclusion of the book, the people are encamped in the plains of Moab opposite Jericho, poised to enter the Promised Land west of the Jordan River. While an initial reading of the book may give the impression of a disorganized conglomeration of material, there is in fact some overall organization to the presentation. And while its confusing stories and ancient ritual legislation may at first seem strange and remote, even such obscure material takes on new meaning as its context is clarified.

THEOLOGICAL THEMES

Numbers is a book about a people on a journey from bondage to freedom. As they journey, the people repeatedly complain about their lot, blame their situation on God and the leaders divinely chosen for them, and find the old days of captivity more enticing than the challenges of moving toward the fulfillment of God's promises to them. The book incorporates some of a larger body of pentateuchal legislation that guided this people in various periods as it sought to maintain its status as a holy community under the leadership of priests and prophets. When the burden of leadership becomes too great, God provides assistants to share the load; nonetheless, the leaders are required to lead the people rightly in reverence for God or risk revocation of their leadership responsibility. Numbers pays special attention to duties of the priests as representatives of the people before God.

Most basic, and undergirding all else, Numbers is a book about God, about the promised yet ever-surprising loyalty of the God who refuses to let go of the people, no matter how rebellious they may be. It is a book about God's provision of material sustenance and leadership, God's acts of intervention on behalf of the people, and God's sustaining blessing of the people as a new generation arises and stands poised at the edge of the Promised Land. As a book about God's care for a people who had a dream but often found themselves too tired or too afraid to move toward the fulfillment of that dream, it is a book for such people in every age.

NAME

The English name "Numbers" is a translation of the title ascribed to this book in the Greek *(Arithmoi)* and later Latin *(Numeri)* translations of the Hebrew Scriptures. This name derives primarily from the records of two occasions on which Moses takes a census of the Israelites (Num. 1–4, 26). Some ancient Jewish traditions also look to the census in referring to Numbers as the "fifth of the numberings" (i.e., the one-fifth of the Torah [Pentateuch] that includes the counting of the people). Although these chapters concerning census-taking are an important key to understanding the organization of the book, they comprise only a minor part of its overall content. The alternative Hebrew name of the book, *Bamidbar* ("in the wilderness"), more clearly suggests the range and interests of the book as a whole.

COMPOSITION

Although there is a long-standing tradition that the entire Pentateuch was composed by Moses, this tradition has been called into question by careful studies of the text ever since the early centuries of the Common Era. Today, most Christian and Jewish scholars believe that the book of Numbers received essentially its present shape during the period of the Babylonian exile (586-539 B.C.E.), after the destruction of Solomon's temple and the city of Jerusalem by King Nebuchadrezzar of Babylon. At that time an anonymous individual or group usually referred to as the Priestly writer(s) (because of their special interest in things pertinent to the priesthood of Israel) prepared an edition of Genesis, Exodus, Leviticus, and Numbers and incorporated older written and oral traditions of the Israelite community. Some of these traditions may go back to the time of Moses; others may have come into existence later and were projected back to the time of Moses. The Priestly writers were concerned with preserving the ancient narrative and legal traditions in such a way that they would have special relevance for the Israelite community in exile in Babylon and could serve as a blueprint for their life in years to come, whether in Babylon or back in their homeland of Judah. This priestly perspective pervades the book of Numbers.

A principal source incorporated by the Priestly writers was the so-called Old Epic tradition. This tradition probably took shape in oral storytelling during the period of the Judges (ca. 1200-1000 B.C.E.) and then was committed to writing during the early period of the Monarchy. There may have been two written versions, one (usually designated J) made in Jerusalem in the era of David and Solomon (1000-922) and another (usually designated E) in the independent kingdom of northern Israel that split off from Jerusalem after Solomon's death. In Numbers it is not generally possible to separate J from E, and some preexilic, non-Priestly materials from other independent traditions seem to have been worked into the text as well. Within Numbers, most of these older materials are incorporated in chs. 10–24. Although some of these older pieces, such as the oracles of Balaam (chs. 23–24), can be readily recognized, other material has been thoroughly reworked by the Priestly editors so that it cannot be neatly sorted out. The volume by Philip J. Budd in the Word Biblical Commentary series offers a convenient summary of scholarly opinions on the sources for each chapter. The present commentary will focus primarily upon the final form of the text, its literary structure, and overall theological themes.

Although the basic shape of the book was established during the Babylonian exile, it seems clear that various materials — sometimes whole chapters, sometimes a few verses or even just a phrase — were added to the text later, probably during the next two hundred years. The Priestly transmitters of the tradition wanted to be sure that the regulations of their own era concerning matters of worship and its leadership, as well as other important matters of community legislation, could be traced to the founders, Moses and Aaron. Unlike today, the custom of those times permitted and even honored such attribution of material to famous personages of the past.

STRUCTURE

All stages of composition described above apply to Genesis through Numbers as a whole, although Leviticus and Numbers contain most of the postexilic additions. In Numbers, especially, this overall process resulted in a book with a seeming hodgepodge of material, jumping from one subject to another, often without a discernible reason for the change in topic. As Dennis Olson *(The Death of the Old and the Birth of the New)* demonstrates in detail, the apparently miscellaneous character of the book has led to great diversity of opinion concerning the outline of Numbers, even in its broadest form. Outlines based on chronology, geography, or thematic considerations lead to various results, and many competing options are possible within each of these main categories.

There is broad agreement that a major break in the narrative occurs at Num. 10:11, with the story of the Israelites' departure from the wilderness of Sinai. Recognition of this break poses, however, two major questions: First, why does the book itself begin in the middle of the Sinai material (which extends back through Leviticus all the way to Exod. 19)? And second, what corresponding division(s) should be identified in the subsequent chapters of Numbers?

With regard to the first question, some scholars have viewed the division between Leviticus and Numbers as purely arbitrary and without significance. But since the breaks between the other pentateuchal books are fairly obviously related to a shift in content (Genesis/Exodus: the death of Joseph; Exodus/Leviticus: the dedication of the tabernacle; Numbers/Deuteronomy: the final speeches of Moses), it seems likely that ancient tradition did regard the first census-taking as a turning point, even though it lay within the traditions associated with Sinai. Olson (48-49) emphasizes that the material of Leviticus is summarized at its conclusion as God's word to Moses "on Mt. Sinai," whereas the opening of Numbers presents God's command to Moses "in the wilderness of Sinai," a significant distinction in locale for the ancient hearer.

The question concerning subdivisions in the remainder of Numbers is more difficult to answer. Most have supposed that another major break corresponding to that at Num. 10:11 comes either at 20:14 (departure from Kadesh in the wilderness) or at 22:1 (the arrival of the people in the plains of Moab). The miscellaneous character of the material in the book as a whole has led to a proliferation of variations on this basic consensus; some scholars would even view an attempt to outline the book as an arbitrary imposition of order upon the miscellany of the book. An alternative approach that cuts through much of the confusion is to concentrate on the two census texts in the book as the key to its structure and organization (Olson). The opening chapter of Numbers enumerates all males of the first generation who are of military age (twenty and older) and ready to march toward the Promised Land. This is followed in chs. 3–4 by a special enumeration of the Levites (who are not counted in the census of the rest of the community). Chapter 26 provides a similar enumeration of adult males ready for battle, followed by enumeration of the Levites. The concluding comment in ch. 26 makes clear that this new census is taken after the first generation has died out during the forty years' wandering occasioned by the people's disobedience:

These were those enrolled by Moses and Eleazar the priest, who enrolled the Israelites in the plains of Moab by the Jordan opposite Jericho. Among these there was not one of those enrolled by Moses and Aaron the priest, who had enrolled the Israelites in the wilderness of Sinai. For the LORD had said of them, "They shall die in the wilderness." Not one of them was left, except Caleb son of Jephunneh and Joshua son of Nun. (26:63-65)

The census itself shows that, while there had been some shifting in the total population of individual tribes, the grand total remained constant at approximately 600,000 persons counted, the traditional number of Exodus participants (aside from women, children, and camp followers) according to Exod. 12:37-38 and Num. 11:21.

According to this analysis, chs. 1–25 present the story of the exodus generation, which rebelled and refused to take the land, and the story of how this generation gradually dies off, partly in the course of judgments for more rebellions. Chapters 26–36 present the story of the successor generation, which is under the same requirement of obedience and is to learn from the fate of its parents. While the first part of the book records the death of everyone except Moses and the two faithful spies Caleb and Joshua, in the second part of the book potential acts of disobedience on the part of the people are averted and no deaths are reported among the Israelites of the new generation.

Most significant of these events involving the second generation is the narrative in ch. 32 of Moses' warning to the Reubenites and Gadites who want to settle in Gilead and not participate with the other tribes in the taking of the land west of the Jordan. Moses reminds them of the dreadful fate (recounted in ch. 14) that befell the spies and indeed the entire previous generation because they failed to take the entire land at God's command. The Reubenites and Gadites swiftly promise to participate fully in the twelve-tribe operation before returning to Gilead. In this text the phrase "from twenty years old and upward" (32:11) is quoted from 14:29 to identify the generation that had been condemned to die in the wilderness for refusing to go up to the

6

land at God's command. This key phrase, used here in a military context, refers explicitly to the group counted in each census, also "from twenty years old and upward . . . able to go to war."

OUTLINE

The preceding observations and a variety of lesser connecting points make it clear that the book should be seen in two parts, chs. 1–25 and 26–36. There are still many possibilities in the subdividing of each major part, however; it seems probable that various transmitters of the tradition viewed the emphases of the story differently, so that the text itself incorporates overlapping outlines.

The difficulties in further subdividing the story are threefold. First and most basic is the tension implicit in the tradition about where the "wilderness" ends and "the land" begins. The question is whether the Israelite territory in Transjordan is to be regarded as part of "the land." All adults of the generation who fled Egypt (except Joshua and Caleb) are supposed to die "in this very wilderness" (14:29). In supposing a two-part division of the book based on the census lists, one would assume that the Israelites who die in the plague recorded in ch. 25 are in fact the last of those adults counted in the first census (although the text never explicitly identifies their generation). Yet at the time of this plague the people are in the plains of Moab and have already taken the Transjordanian territories of Sihon and Og, which will subsequently be allotted to the tribes of Reuben and Gad and half of Manasseh. To reconcile the time of the ending of the first generation with the time of Israel's entrance into the land, one must assume that "the land" does not include Transjordan, but only the territory west of the Jordan River, even though Israelite tribes lived in Transjordan. This point of view is indeed presented in the boundary summary of ch. 34, where the eastern boundary is given as the Jordan River; it is also conspicuous in other biblical texts (e.g., Josh. 5:12, which records that the manna ceased after the people had crossed the Jordan). Once the capture of Transjordan is thus eliminated from the "land" tradition and attached to the "wilderness" tradition geographically as well as chronologically, there remains no one geographical subdivision of singular importance either for the beginning of the attempt to enter the land from the east (Num. 20:14 or 22) or for the arrival in the plains of Moab as a staging ground for taking "the land" (22:1). Alternatively, one may ignore geography altogether and organize chs. 1–25 around the theme of disobedience or around the theme of leadership.

The second major difficulty in outlining the text lies in the miscellaneous character and seemingly random location of the legal materials found in Numbers. As can be seen in the outline below, these laws are found in chs. 5–6, 15, 19, 27, 28–30, 35, and 36. Itinerary lists and instructions for priestly duties are also scattered through the narrative material in a way that seems to defy modern logic. A variety of explanations has been offered in rabbinic tradition and in modern scholarship, but all seem to be ad hoc.

Third, chs. 26–36 overall give the impression of a series of appendixes, despite the structure provided by the two-census pattern. The separation of the two narrative/legal texts concerning the daughters of Zelophehad (chs. 27 and 36), the commissioning of Joshua before the end of Moses' military leadership (27:12-23), the view of Balaam in 31:16 (so different from his portrayal in chs. 22–24), and the disproportionate amount of legislative material all support the view that much of chs. 26–36 consists of additions to the basic core of the book.

In light of the many complications, the outline that follows offers just one of many possible approaches. Anyone who studies Numbers should take up the challenge of outlining the book, if only to discover the problems involved.

Part One: The First Wilderness Generation

(Those who left Egypt under Moses' leadership)

A. Preparation for journeying from Sinai (1:1–10:10).

    1. Census of all the congregation; arrangements for order of encampment and order of march (1:1–2:34).

2. Special role of the Levites between the whole congregation and the Aaronic priests; census of the Levites (3:1–4:49).

3. Miscellaneous legislation covering skin diseases, restitution in damages cases, women suspected of adultery, nazirite vows (5:1–6:21; the logic of this collection and its placement is not clear).

4. Aaronic benediction (6:22-27).

5. Review of offerings given at the dedication of the tabernacle (7:1-89; this dedication, recorded in Exod. 40, and also the materials in Num. 8–9, are said to have taken place prior to the census of Num. 1–4).

6. Consecration of the Levites, prior to the census (8:1-26).

7. Concerning the Passover celebrated at the dedication of the tabernacle, prior to the census (9:1-14).

8. Anticipatory description of encamping and breaking camp by the sign of the cloud over the tabernacle; silver trumpets for official signals to leaders and people (9:15–10:10).

B. Journey from the wilderness of Sinai to the plains of Moab opposite Jericho (10:11–21:35).

1. The march commences according to the instruction of chs. 2–3 (10:11-28).

2. Old traditions concerning Moses' father-in-law, the ark of the covenant (10:29-36).

3. Stories about proper leadership (11:1–20:13).

   (a) The people's desire for meat; the sharing of Moses' leadership with seventy elders (11:1-35).

   (b) Miriam and Aaron challenge Moses' special relationship to God and are rebuffed (12:1-16).

   (c) Spies sent into Canaan bring back a discouraging report, leading to rebellion of the people. God intends to disinherit the people completely, but Moses intercedes on their behalf. God forgives the community, but declares that none of this generation "twenty years old and upward" shall enter the land, except the two faithful spies Caleb and Joshua (13:1–14:45).

(d) Miscellaneous legislation concerning various offerings, sabbath violation, tassels on garments as reminder of commandments (15:1-41; the logic of this collection and its placement not clear).

(e) Challenges to Aaron's leadership; Aaronic priesthood confirmed by almond blossoms on his rod; responsibilities of Aaronic priests and the Levites (16:1–18:32).

(f) Ritual of the red heifer: purification in cases of contact with dead bodies (19:1-22; the logic of this placement not clear).

(g) Death of Miriam; failure of good leadership on the part of Moses and Aaron means that they cannot lead the people into the land but must die in the wilderness with the first generation (20:1-13).

4. Travel from Kadesh to the plains of Moab: death of Aaron and Eleazar's succession to priestly leadership; battle at Arad; fiery serpents; Sihon and Og (20:14–21:35).

C. End of the first generation in the plains of Moab opposite Jericho (22:1–25:18).

1. Balaam, hired by King Balak of Moab to curse Israel, can only bless Israel because God has blessed the people (22:1–24:25).

2. Israel's apostasy in contact with Moabites and Midianites leads to the death of the last of the first generation (25:1-18).

Part Two: The Second Wilderness Generation

(Those who will later enter the land under Joshua's leadership)

A. Census of the new generation, with indication that the census will be the basis for land distribution; census of the Levites (26:1-65).

B. Miscellaneous collection of legislation and narrative covering all events prior to the final speeches of Moses and his death, which are reported in the book of Deuteronomy (27:1–36:13).

1. The daughters of Zelophehad and regulations concerning women's land inheritance (27:1-11).

2. Commissioning of Joshua as Moses' eventual successor (27:12-23).

3. Miscellaneous legislation concerning offerings, festivals, validity of women's vows (28:1–30:16; the logic of this collection and its placement not clear).

4. War against Midian (following command given in 25:17) and distribution of booty (31:1-54).

5. Allotment of territory in Transjordan to Reuben, Gad, and half the tribe of Manasseh (32:1-42).

6. Summary of itinerary from Egypt to the plains of Moab (33:1-56).

7. Matters concerning land distribution (34:1–36:13).

   (a) Summary of the boundaries of the Promised Land; appointment of the leaders who will apportion the land to the tribes (34:1-29).

   (b) Instruction that the (landless) Levites shall be apportioned cities with pasturage (35:1-8).

   (c) Designation of cities of refuge for persons who commit homicide; regulation for use of these cities (35:9-34).

   (d) The daughters of Zelophehad and tribal marriage restriction for women who inherit land (36:1-13).

VALUE AS A HISTORICAL SOURCE

Although scholars have questioned all parts of Numbers as reliable information for the period prior to the emergence of Israel in Canaan, many individual texts probably developed from historical circumstances in various periods of the people's past. Perhaps the most basic question is whether or not a twelve-tribe structure existed during the wilderness period. To answer this question, the historical validity of the overall narrative structure of the Pentateuch must be assessed. Did one family (twelve sons, seventy persons; Gen. 46:8-27) go down to Egypt in the time of Jacob and blossom to twelve full-scale tribes, 600,000 men, by the time of Moses? Did all these people leave Egypt to gradually die out over forty years in the wilderness, and did the successive generation arrive in equal strength opposite Jericho?

Scholars agree widely that the biblical account presents an idealized and generalized portrait of the background of the people of Israel in the land. Most do not accept the assumption of a twelve-tribe structure for the historical group that left Egypt and experienced the adventures of the wilderness. Indeed, some would question even whether the tribes came together formally in a group of twelve during the period of the judges, suggesting instead that the twelve-tribe system was a construct developed for administrative purposes during the reign of King David (ca. 1000 B.C.E.). Thus neither the listing of the tribes in the two census documents nor the total population figures given reflect the wilderness situation. It seems more likely that some groups who made up Israel during the period of the judges recalled stories of desert life and perhaps of battles engaged in, and that these stories became a part of the Old Epic tradition of the whole community. Even in the twentieth century C.E., anthropologists have found tribal groups who have forged a common identity through a process in which the stories of various individual clans and tribes are adopted as the stories of everyone in the community. It is somewhat like the way that people in the United States have adopted the old Thanksgiving story of the New England Pilgrims as a national holiday, and thus all the people's heritage, even though the people have come from many different ethnic

12

backgrounds and arrived in the United States over several centuries.

Although it is difficult to state with certainty what happened in the wilderness, it is reasonable to assume that a group of oppressed slaves fled Egypt under Moses, gained a new or renewed religious identity, and moved through the Sinai Peninsula to Transjordan. The date is difficult to fix precisely, and the tradition of forty years wandering should probably not be taken as an exact figure. Sometime during the thirteenth century B.C.E. seems the most likely period in which to place the movement from Egypt to Canaan. It also seems reasonable to assume that Moses did play the key leadership role, despite the argument by some scholars (e.g., Martin Noth, *A History of Pentateuchal Traditions*) that Moses did not have a significant place in the original events. The people who fled Egypt into the barren wastes of the Sinai Peninsula may have eaten manna (probably a sweet sticky excretion of scale insects that can still be gathered today in the Sinai), perhaps quail also (the birds drop exhausted on the ground after migratory flight across the Mediterranean), and may have seen water come from a break in hard-surfaced limestone rock. It is possible that some of them participated in battles at places such as Arad/Hormah (Num. 21:1-3; cf. 14:45) or in the area of Heshbon (21:21-25), although archaeological work has not been able to confirm such events. It is possible that this group remained in the wilderness for a full generation, but it should be noted that the text itself suggests that most of this time was spent at the oasis of Kadesh, some fifty miles southeast of Beer-sheba. And yet establishment of such details, if it were possible, still would not bring one to the heart of the story. For Numbers is most of all a story about a people and its leadership and its God, and how the three interact. The theological core of meaning in this story is simply not verifiable by the methods of historical inquiry.

Many scholars believe that the text reflects traditions of two different groups who entered the land separately. One of these, associated especially with the name of Caleb and the area around Hebron, entered from the south. Its story, told in Num. 14, now takes the form of an abortive effort, because the story of the arrival through Transjordan (chs. 20–25) became normative for the later community.

The passages describing duties of priests and Levites probably reflect various stages in the development of Israel's priesthood, especially the late period. Likewise, the regulations concerning festivals and sacrifices show development through many phases, especially when studied in connection with related texts in Exodus, Leviticus, and Deuteronomy. Much on such subjects that appears in Numbers probably relates to worship in the Second Temple after 515 B.C.E. and thus belongs to the "post-P" supplements of the text (see above, Composition). The other legislation scattered throughout Numbers is also likely to represent traditions of varying date and background.

Some of the disputes about leadership may go back to events of the wilderness period, but all have been extensively edited to reflect concerns of later generations. The story of the seventy elders and the prophesying of Eldad and Medad (Num. 11:26-30), for example, focuses on the possibility of prophecy outside regular channels, an issue of great concern in the era of the Monarchy. So also the story of Aaron and Miriam's challenge to Moses (Num. 12) probably reflects controversies between competing religious groups during the monarchical period. The period(s) and nature of the controversies between the Levites and the priesthood of the line of Aaron are much debated, but, again, concerns reflected in the text seem to relate to the Second Temple period and perhaps also to some degree to the reign of King Josiah (640-609).

UNDERSTANDING THE PRIESTHOOD OF ANCIENT ISRAEL

Much of the book of Numbers deals with priests of the line of Aaron and a group called Levites with its various subdivisions. Aaron and Moses were both members of the tribe of Levi, but the priestly line of Aaron is carefully distinguished from the Levites; therefore, the place and role of these two groups in the history of Israel's religious leadership present special problems. These problems are reviewed briefly here as a background for the treatment of specific texts in the Commentary section.

While Julius Wellhausen's classic treatment of the history of Israel's priesthood (*Prolegomena to the History of Israel*, 121-151) continues to exercise great influence, important new studies have appeared in the last fifty years. The various contemporary reconstructions of the history of the Israelite priesthood offer differing bases from which to approach interpretation of a whole series of texts in Numbers. Although some of these texts themselves form part of the evidence for the history of the priesthood, the evidence involves texts from diverse parts of the Pentateuch, Samuel, Ezekiel, Ezra, Chronicles, and other books as well. Scholars identify three important problems in this biblical evidence. First, the relationship between Levites and Aaronic priests is unclear in the tradition as a whole, and seems to have evolved especially between the seventh and fifth centuries B.C.E. Second, the relationship of the Zadokite priesthood (established by David in Jerusalem and growing in power in the succeeding centuries) to the "line of Aaron" is not clear from the biblical text and must be reconstructed. Finally, there are hints of a priesthood related to the lineage of Moses that need to be explained.

The texts in Numbers of particular significance for this discussion include chs. 3–4, giving the lineage of Aaron, the census of the Levites, and their various sanctuary duties; ch. 8, describing the consecration ceremony for Levites (in contrast to a ceremony for Aaronic priests in Lev. 8); ch. 12, Aaron and Miriam's challenge to Moses; chs. 16–18, Korah's challenge to Aaron, the confirmation of Aaronic authority, and the separate duties and rights of Aaronic priests and other Levites; ch. 25, the vindication of Phinehas; and 26:57-62, the second levitical census.

The reconstructions made by two scholars will serve to illustrate the problems. Aelred Cody (*A History of Old Testament Priesthood*, iv-v) argues that neither Moses nor Aaron is depicted as a priestly figure in the Old Epic tradition. Moreover, in line with many other scholars, Cody believes that the Zadokites of the Jerusalem temple had no historical tribal connection to Aaron or to the Levites; he views the connection portrayed in biblical texts as a late fiction created by the Zadokites to establish their claim to continuous authority. According to Cody's analysis, Aaron was a popular figure in southern Judah and some members of the tribe of Levi began to trace their ancestry to him. In the seventh century B.C.E., King Josiah centralized worship in Jerusalem and closed local shrines in the countryside. At that time some of the Levites who had functioned as priests at such shrines sought admission to the priesthood at the Jerusalem temple but were rebuffed by the Zadokites. In the aftermath of the Babylonian exile, the traditional "preference" that all priests should be of levitical extraction arose and prompted the Zadokites to claim the southern Levites' Aaron as their ancestor as well. Some Levites who had been local priests did become officiants at altar sacrifices along with the Zadokites, but most were relegated to secondary duties of care for the temple equipment. These were called "levites"; the use of the lowercase in English indicates a change in the connotation of the Hebrew term: what had long designated tribal membership (Levite) comes to describe instead a person with particular temple duties (levite).

Frank Moore Cross *(Canaanite Myth and Hebrew Epic),* by contrast, views Aaron as a priestly figure in the Old Epic traditions and regards Moses as the ancestral head of a priestly house as well. Cross argues that the Zadokites present an ancient lineage of Aaronids centered in Hebron whom King David installed in Jerusalem alongside the Mushite (from Moses) line of Abiathar. Solomon's dismissal of Abiathar (1 Kgs. 2:26-27) led to the gradual ascendancy of the Zadokite line. King Jeroboam of the schismatic northern kingdom imitated David's religious policies, according to Cross, by establishing a Mushite priesthood in Dan and an Aaronic priesthood in Bethel (Cody regards the priesthood of Dan as levitical but not Mushite, and rejects any historical connection of an Aaronic line with Bethel). Since Cross's focus is on the early period, he does not detail the emergence of the postexilic picture of priests and levites in the Jerusalem temple. Clearly the process would be simpler than that pictured by Cody, since the Zadokites are regarded as Aaronids from the beginning.

On the model of either analysis, the Priestly material in the story of Korah's revolt (Num. 16) can best be understood as a levitical protest overruled by priestly (Zadokite) interests in the period when the Zadokites were consolidating their claims and the "levitical" status of other temple functionaries was emerging.

16

Both interpretations of the priesthood would recognize the post-exilic distinction between Aaronic priests and subordinate levites in the duty and offering requirements detailed in ch. 18.

The alternative reconstructions of the priesthood make a significant difference, however, for the interpretation of ch. 12. Cody argues that the story shows no priestly traits in Aaron's behavior, since Aaron's intercession for Miriam is with his brother Moses, not with God, and since the shutting out of persons with skin disease is not restricted to the priesthood (*A History of Old Testament Priesthood*, 150). Cross, by contrast, offers no comment on such details but focuses instead on larger themes of the passage. He finds that the text highlights "(1) Moses' superiority to the house of Aaron as mediator of the divine command, and (2) the affirmation of the legitimacy of the Mushite priesthood despite its 'mixed' blood" (*Canaanite Myth and Hebrew Epic*, 204).

Divergent interpretations of the genealogical information in chs. 3 and 26 are quite technical, and any study of this complex topic is somewhat speculative. On the whole, Cross's approach offers a better rationale for the preservation of stories such as ch. 12 over centuries of tradition. Most important is to understand the general point that neither the narratives nor the more technical priestly information about the levitical families can be interpreted apart from some comprehensive view of Israel's priesthood.

HOLINESS IN THE PRIESTLY TRADITION

Two kinds of distinctions may be recognized within Israel's conception of holiness: a distinction between the sacred (or holy) and the profane (or common), and a distinction between what is pure (clean) and what is impure (unclean). Although these distinctions can be said to undergird all of Israel's life as a sacral community, they play an explicit role in numerous passages in the book of Numbers. Chapters in which the first distinction (sacred/profane) is prominent include 3–4, 6, 8, 16–18, and 28–29. Chapters concerned with purity/impurity include 5, 9, 19, 31, and 35. As J. Gammie *(Holiness in Israel)* has shown, holiness is viewed differently in the prophetic traditions, in wisdom literature, and in various representatives of priestly circles such as the Holiness code or Ezekiel. The material in Numbers reflects the concerns associated with the so-called Priestly strand of the Pentateuch (see above, p. 3), and the background information summarized here is restricted to that perspective.

The distinction between sacred and profane in this priestly tradition has to do with setting apart some things or persons from others, so that sacred space (where God is especially present) and sacred personages (often but not always responsible for sacrifices in the sacred space) are identified. The setting apart or consecration is accomplished by various one-time rituals and signified by various continuing practices. The tabernacle and its appurtenances are set apart by an initial special dedicatory ritual (Exod. 40), for example; its sacred status is then continuously signified by the sacred status of the Levites designated to carry it (Num. 3–4), as well as by the entire pattern of the order of encampment and marching in the wilderness (ch. 2).

So also various classes of persons may be set apart by ritual. The rites for consecration of the priests are specified in Lev. 8–9, those for the Levites in Num. 8. The narratives and instructions of chs. 16–18 suggest that eligibility for such consecration and its meaning for the special duties or privileges of those set apart as priests or Levites were matters of dispute in the history of the people. While these two classes appear to have involved consecration for a lifetime, persons called Nazirites were set apart for specified periods of time (Num. 6). The attention to the ritual for de-consecrating the Nazirite at the end of the specified time period further highlights the importance of marking the boundaries between the sacred and the profane.

Along with sacred space and sacred persons or groups, the category of sacred times should also be noted. In the priestly tradition the sabbath is treated as a holy day, and certain other festivals are described as "holy convocations" (chs. 28–29). The fact that these days are holy because they are so designated by God lifts up the theological reality that the holiness of sacred persons and sacred spaces is likewise conferred by God, who is quintessentially holy and who alone is the source of all holiness.

Scholars are widely agreed that Israel's view of holiness incorporated a notion of degrees or levels. Thus the priests are more holy than the Levites, as can be seen by their special duties regarding the ark and the equipment of the tabernacle (Num. 4). Indeed, the priestly tradition does not use the Hebrew technical term "holy" *(qadosh)* with reference to the Levites (contrast Num. 8 to Lev. 8; see Jacob Milgrom, *Leviticus 1–16*, 49). This gradation of holiness is further evidenced by the regulations of Num. 18 that restrict access to the altar and sanctuary utensils to the priests alone and that distinguish the offerings for priestly consumption from those permitted to the Levites. Reciprocally, the sanctuary itself is perceived to have "zones" of holiness, with the innermost area to be entered only by the high priest (Lev. 16), the altar service reserved to the priesthood generally, and an outer area for levitical service.

The second major dimension of holiness focuses on distinguishing between pure and impure conditions, together with rituals for cleansing from impurity. Impurity of individuals or objects could result from contact with a dead body (Num. 19) or with an animal defined by Israel as "unclean" (Lev. 11). Individual impurity was also associated with certain skin diseases (Lev. 13; Num. 12), with bodily emissions (semen or menstrual blood, Lev. 15; Num. 5), or with childbirth (Lev. 12). Houses and objects in them could also become unclean by analogy to skin disease (Lev. 14) and thus be in need of ritual purification.

The criteria for distinguishing between pure and impure conditions (and also between clean and unclean animals) are not self-evident. Anthropologist Mary Douglas *(Purity and Danger)* has proposed that matter "out of place" is the central criterion for uncleanness, and this analysis is widely followed concerning the distinctions among animals made in Leviticus. With regard to the causes of impurity in human beings, however, more must be said. There are four polluting factors (death, blood, semen, and skin disease), and as Milgrom suggests (*Numbers,* 346), these factors have the common denominator of death. Thus they are perceived to stand in opposition to God, the Holy One and the author of life. In her more recent work, Douglas agrees with Milgrom that with regard to impurity in Numbers, "The underlying principle is that death and life are opposed" (*In the Wilderness,* 23).

Those who are impure must be separated from the rest of the community until a cure of disease (if relevant) and proper cleansing rituals have been accomplished (Num. 5, 12, 19, 31). In cases of disease, the rites of purification do not bring about healing, but are carried out only after healing is already complete. The physical separation from the rest of the community is intended to prevent the impure from coming into contact with what is holy; thus there is an interconnection between the pure/impure distinction and the sacred (holy)/profane (common) distinction. This interconnection can be seen, for instance, in the requirement that the period of the Nazirite's vow must be re-served in its entirety if the consecrated person becomes impure during the period of the vow (Num. 6).

A further connection between pure/impure and holy/common arises in the understanding of Israel's sin offerings, which are also understood as purification offerings. Although the precise purpose of these sin (or purification) offerings within Israel's sacrificial system remains debated, it is clear that impurity can result from sin, as well as from the physical factors mentioned above, and that the impurity caused by sin could pollute the sanctuary as well as the sinful community.

Finally, the social significance of this priestly treatment of impurity should not go unnoticed. During the postexilic period many Israelites held negative views of outsiders. Douglas (*In the Wilderness*) points out that in the impurity texts of Numbers defilement comes from *within* the community, either through physical conditions to which anyone may be subject or through sin. Defilement is *not*, however, defined as coming from contact with outsiders. Thus Douglas argues that the purity traditions of Numbers (along with other features of the book) were developed in opposition to the xenophobic views of Judah's leadership in the era of Ezra and Nehemiah. In our own era, so characterized by ethnic hatred and warfare, Douglas's interpretation deserves serious attention for its theological implications as well as for its anthropological insight.*

* Apart from the section on Holiness, the Introduction is excerpted with permission of Charles Scribner's Sons, an imprint of Macmillan Publishing Company, from my article, "Numbers," in *The Books of the Bible,* Bernhard W. Anderson, editor, Vol. 1, pp. 71-87. Copyright © 1989 Charles Scribner's Sons.

PREPARATION FOR
JOURNEYING FROM SINAI
(1:1–10:10)

CHAPTER 1

The book of Numbers opens with God's command to Moses to take a census of the Israelite males aged twenty and above. The tribal representatives who are to assist Moses are named by God. Moses and Aaron, with these assistants, conduct the census, and the results are recorded.

1:1-47   The date given in 1:1 connects the narrative chronologically to Exod. 40:17. One month has elapsed since the setting up and dedication of the "tabernacle," here referred to as the "tent of meeting" (Num. 1:1). In Exod. 40 both terms are used, as well as the combined phrase "tabernacle of the tent of meeting." Tabernacle and tent of meeting were two different names by which Israelite tradition remembered the sacred tent of the wilderness era; probably "tent of meeting" was the older name. Details of its construction, probably reflecting a later era, are given in Exod. 26–27 and 36–38.

The location "in the wilderness of Sinai" used in combination with the tent of meeting reflects a new phase of Israel's wilderness experience. Exodus 19:1 announces the arrival of the people at the wilderness of Sinai, and the focus from then onward is on Israel's presence before the mountain of Sinai. Although the book of Leviticus begins with God's speech to Moses from the newly dedicated tent of meeting, it ends with a summary reference to commands given "on Mount Sinai" (Lev. 27:34). Numbers now takes up the topic of preparations for life after departure from the wilderness of Sinai by introducing arrangements for the line of march (Num. 10:11ff.). These further instructions are given through Moses "in the wilderness of Sinai," not "on Mount Sinai." The first step of such arrangements is the census.

This census has important functions in the structure of the book of Numbers as a whole. Together with the second census in ch. 26, it serves to mark off two major periods and groups of the wilderness era. The first census is an accounting of those who originally departed from Egypt; the second is an accounting of the second generation Israelites who after the forty years in the wilderness are those who will enter the Promised Land. The book of Numbers can be outlined in various ways. The basic division in the book, however, is between these two generations. Both generations are approximately equal in total population, although the count for each tribe varies. The final form of the Numbers narrative as a whole presents the original generation who left Egypt as repeatedly disobeying God. This is in contrast to the second generation, which is characterized by perfect obedience (Dennis Olson, *The Death of the Old*).

The text is explicit that only males are counted in this census, and there are indications that a military census is meant. The age group counted is repeatedly identified as "everyone in Israel able to go to war." Some scholars also suggest that the word translated "thousands" had a secondary meaning of "military unit" that may have applied here. If that is correct, it is possible that the actual numbers represented in the census figures for each tribe are only the hundreds listed at the end of each count. Reuben, for example, would be counted at forty-six units totaling five hundred men (1:21). The resulting lower figures would fit better with archaeologists' estimates of the population of premonarchic Israel. Alternatively, the high figures (more than 603,000 adult males) may be a projection into the wilderness era from the era of the Monarchy. Whatever the actual number, the narrator wants to emphasize God's amazing sustaining of so many people under the difficult and dangerous wilderness conditions, so that the second generation is the same size as the first. In a world where population stability (rather than growth) was the norm and where decimation by famine was well known, the very numbers of the census counts proclaim the power and grace of Israel's God.

1:48-54   Beginning at 1:48, we learn that the tribe of Levi is to be treated differently from the others. Israel's two ways of naming its twelve tribes can be seen in this chapter. Anyone reading the list of assistants in vv. 5-15 would assume that the twelve tribes included the names Ephraim and Manasseh and would know nothing of a tribe named Levi. Only the introduction to v. 10, "from the sons of Joseph," might give a clue to the attentive reader that these two, as descendants of one father, are different from the others in the initial list. Whenever Levi is to be counted among the twelve, Ephraim and Manasseh are treated as subunits of a single tribe, so that the total of twelve is undisturbed. In this chapter we see the two ways of counting side by side and only thinly accommodated to each other by the introductory phrases in vv. 10 and 32.

Delaying any mention of the Levites until the end of the chapter provides a transition to the following chapters. We are told in vv. 48-54 that the Levites will have special responsibility for the tabernacle, while the other tribes have general guard duty (v. 52). Chapters 2–4 then provide the details of these arrangements.

CHAPTER 2

The tribes are assigned to locations where they should encamp
(2:2); the same locations are to be maintained during the people's
movement from one place to another (v. 17). At the center is the
tent of meeting, with three tribes on each side. The named heads
of each tribe are the same as those mentioned in 1:4-15 as Moses
and Aaron's assistants in the census. The order in which the tribes
are listed, however, is different from the census. By listing Judah
first and by placing Judah in the traditionally more sacred eastern
position, the writer alludes to the preeminence of this tribe in the
history of the people. Judah was King David's tribe. It was the
center of the southern kingdom. In postexilic times the people
of Judah regarded themselves as the remnant of the true people
of God in contrast to the people in the area of the old northern
kingdom.

The central position of the sacred tent and the language used
in the chapter suggest both religious and military connotations
for this order of encampment and march. The language of "regi-
ments," "companies," and "ensigns" (NRSV) clearly reflects the
military motif. At the same time, the overall design of the camp
and the emphasis that each tribe must face the tent of meeting
make clear the sacral nature of this arrangement. This arrangement
may reflect an ancient pilgrimage tradition. The military and
religious motifs reflect the conception of wilderness Israel both
as a sacred community and as a community encountering enemies
(e.g., 21:1-3). Religious festivals and military action were certainly
separable in Israel's history. The close connection between religious observance and battle led by their God is nevertheless
evident in many narratives in the books of Joshua, Judges, and

26

Samuel. Examples of this connection include the story of Jericho in Josh. 6, the story of Gideon in Judg. 6, and the Ark narratives of 1 Sam. 4–7.

The theme of the special status of the Levites, introduced in Num. 1, is reiterated twice in this chapter. The Levites appear in 2:17, assigned to the center location with the sacred tent. Appropriately, the location of this reference to the Levites is in the literary center of the list, between the assignments for the first six tribes and the remaining six. In vv. 32-33, the writer's summary calls attention to the lack of a numerical total for the Levitical regiment in v. 17. This reminds the reader that in obedience to divine command (1:49) Levi had not been counted. As in ch. 1 (see above), the naming of the twelve tribes here excludes Levi.

The concluding emphasis of this chapter is that the Israelites did "just as the LORD had commanded Moses" (2:33, 34). This theme has appeared already in 1:54 and appears repeatedly in much of what scholars have identified as the "Priestly" (P) contribution to the Pentateuch (see Introduction). In some examples, as here, the obedient action is simply summarized. In other cases, notably the construction of the tabernacle in the concluding chapters of Exodus, the carrying out of the divine command is spelled out in full detail, with extensive repetition. This emphasis on exact obedience wherever it occurs provides the backdrop against which the text portrays the seriousness of the people's sin when they act on their own or disobey divine directives.

CHAPTER 3

The special status of the Levites having been established generally in chs. 1 and 2, attention is now given to their subdivisions and their special duties with regard to the tent of meeting. The chapter opens, however, with a brief paragraph about the priesthood of the line of Aaron.

3:1-4   There is a tension between the topic of Aaron's descendants and the main theme of the chapter in 3:5ff. This tension points to a crux of scholarly debate about the history of Israel's religious leadership, its structure and hierarchy. It is generally agreed that this structure did change and evolve over the span of about twelve hundred years from Moses to the fall of the Second Temple in 70 C.E. The OT texts from various periods often draw on more ancient traditions. Because of this, it is not clear whether a priesthood tracing its descent from Aaron was an early or late development. It is also not easy to discern how such a priesthood related to the category of Levites (see Introduction). The overall tradition preserved ascribes the most important duties to the Aaronic priesthood, with lesser responsibilities assigned to the group known as Levites (see vv. 5ff.). It is possible, however, that this assignment of secondary roles for the Levites emerged as late as the reform of King Josiah, or even during the postexilic period.

Verses 1-4 are appropriate to the context, however, because Moses is remembered as a child of Levitical parentage (Exod. 2; 6:20) and Aaron is remembered as brother of Moses (Exod. 6:20). The listing of Aaron's sons similarly follows the traditional genealogy of Exod. 6:23. The story of the death of Nadab and

Abihu (v. 4) for making an offering not specifically commanded by the LORD is recorded briefly in Lev. 10.

3:5-13   Verses 5-10 establish the specific role of the Levites as assistants to the Aaronic line, and introduce the Levites' responsibilities for the furnishings of the tent. Before detailing these duties, however, the writer introduces in vv. 11-13 the understanding of the Levites as substitute for sacrifice of the Israelite firstborn (males). This idea, which 8:5-19 develops ceremonially, is a reminder of the story of the first Passover (Exod. 12–13). It gives the Levites sacred status; they are not at all to be viewed as casual functionaries or custodians. Exodus 13:13 indicates that the firstborn male child is not to be killed but "redeemed," even as God redeemed Israel as a whole from Egypt. The Exodus text does not specify how this redemption is to be symbolized or enacted; Num. 3 and 8 provide these details and offer a theological interpretation.

Despite this high view of the Levites as a substitute for the firstborn, however, the warning of 3:10 against any who would wrongly claim for themselves Aaronic responsibilities may be directed especially toward the Levitical group. Ancient debates are reflected here. These ancient debates are about whom God has chosen or called. They are about the duties or privileges of those ordained, and about the limitations on the prerogatives of other leaders or laypersons.

3:14-39   The paragraphs of vv. 14-39 summarize the enrollment of the Levitical clans and give a summary statement of their assignments. A census is taken of the ancestral houses of the Gershonites, Kohathites, and Merarites, the descendants of Levi's three sons (v. 17). This enumeration of the Levites differs from that of the other tribes in ch. 1, and thus it does not violate the divine command (1:48-49) that Levi not be numbered as the other tribes. The Levites are not counted from the age of twenty and up (and thus based on military status) as are the other tribes; instead they are counted "from a month old," the age at which redemption of a firstborn male is required (vv. 40-41).

With respect to the tabernacle, the Gershonites are to camp

29

on the west (v. 23), the Kohathites on the south (v. 29), and the Merarites on the north (v. 35). Not surprisingly, Moses and Aaron and Aaron's sons are given the place of preeminence on the eastern side of the tabernacle (v. 38). This fills out the fourth side, although the number of persons on the east would be far less than for the other three sides. Although the text never specifies the placement of these leaders in relation to the whole people, one must presume that these four groups encamped close to the tent, while the assignments for the twelve tribes' encampment given in ch. 2 were further away from the holy area. Numbers 3:32 designates Eleazar, son of Aaron, as head over the other three leaders of the Levites. Perhaps his role is mentioned here, rather than in v. 38 where his encampment location is given, because of the reference in v. 31 to the ark and the most sacred equipment "with which the priests minister."

The number of Levites given in the Hebrew text for each of the three main groups (vv. 22, 28, 34) adds up to 22,300, not the 22,000 given in v. 39. This discrepancy becomes important in seeking to understand the next section, which presumes the summary number of 22,000. One tradition of Greek manuscripts reads 8,300 in v. 28 (rather than the 8,600 of the Hebrew), which makes the final total add up correctly. It is, however, difficult to say whether this Greek tradition is an original reading, or whether it was introduced to harmonize an awkward text.

3:40-51   Verses 40-51 report the establishment of the redemptive role of the Levites announced in vv. 11-13 and expand that role to cover livestock as well as human beings. There are tensions in the text that suggest layering of traditions here. No approved human sacrifice is known in Israel's history. The sacrifice of firstborn animals, which seems to be removed here at least on a one-time basis, was apparently practiced even in the postexilic era. Further, the number 22,273 is awkward in relation to the census results of ch. 2. It has been calculated that this small number of firstborn would mean that each family recorded in ch. 2 would have an average of forty adult males. The divine instruction that the remaining 273 firstborn (presuming a total of 22,000 Levites) must be redeemed by prescribed financial payment leaves further questions unanswered. From which individuals exactly and on what basis were the needed 1,365 shekels to be collected? Perhaps the purpose of this section is to be seen in v. 48: monetary redemption provides a source of income for the Aaronic priesthood. The price of five shekels corresponds to the amount specified in Lev. 27:6 as the equivalent for a male human being age one month to five years.

The need for this redemption of firstborn Israelite males and their cattle is connected in Num. 3:13 to the context of the final plague in Egypt. In this plague the firstborn sons and firstborn cattle of the Egyptians were struck down (Exod. 12:29). God's claim in Num. 3:13 is anticipated by Exod. 13:2 and the instructions for redemption in Exod. 13:11-16. As is usual for Israel's androcentric and patrilineal culture, the birth of females is not of ritual significance. The text is concerned strictly with males and their value as a substitution for other males. Nonetheless, the larger tradition of redemption both establishes differences between humans and animals, thus precluding child sacrifice, and emphasizes the importance of new life as a gift from God.

The substitution of Levites for firstborn males also connects every family in principle to the special service performed by the Levites as God's designated hereditary group responsible for religious rites. Thus in Israel ordinary families are not expected to present their firstborn for sanctuary service (Samuel is an exception because of Hannah's vow in 1 Sam. 1). Rather this duty is given to the Levites both as representatives of the people and as a sanctified buffer group between the ordinary Israelites and the holiness of the deity.

CHAPTER 4

A new enumeration of the three Levitical groups counted in ch. 3 is made at God's command; this enumeration considers only those between thirty and fifty years of age. In this context the procedures for taking down, packing up, and carrying the tent sanctuary and its contents are specified in greater detail. The text does not give an explanation for the age range of thirty to fifty years for this enumeration. It is reasonable to suppose that younger adults may have been expected to serve a training period for this important sacred work. It is also reasonable that strength for the physical work required suggested an upper age limit.

As with ch. 3, the enumeration is preceded by attention to the role of the Aaronic group (4:5-14); as in previous passages, the text makes clear the higher standing of Aaron and his descendants with regard to the sacred objects. The Aaronids are responsible for dismantling and wrapping all of the objects in the central sanctuary, as well as for attaching the carrying poles. Only then may the Kohathite group of Levites approach; the Kohathites are not even to look upon the sacred objects (v. 20). The Gershonites and Merarites, as anticipated in ch. 3, carry the outer parts of the tabernacle.

The description of the tabernacle and its equipment is abbreviated here, and one might suppose that it was easily portable. The detailed plans given in Exod. 25–27 and 36–38, however, describe a large and heavy structure. Most scholars therefore question whether the sanctuary as described in Exodus was in use during the wilderness period. Whatever the origins of the descriptions of the tabernacle, the final form of the tradition draws our attention to its value in terms of materials used, to its beauty, and most of all to its sacredness as the place where the community encountered the holy God.

CHAPTER 5

Numbers 5 offers the first strong indication of the miscellaneous character of the final form of much of the book of Numbers. The theme of enumeration is at an end, but the theme of the tabernacle and the Levites is abruptly dropped, to be resumed in chs. 7–8. Chapter 5 offers a miscellany of regulations for the purity of the Israelite community, moving from uncleanness to wrong behavior to suspicion of adultery. In the first two cases, the text makes specific its reference to both men and women as equally subject to the regulation, a relatively rare specification in Hebrew law. In the third regulation, by contrast, while both male and female are involved, they are not at all comparably treated.

5:1-4   Persons affected by three different types of uncleanness are to be put outside the camp, so that the community among whom the holy God dwells will not be made impure (v. 3). Each of these categories of uncleanness is dealt with in more detail elsewhere in the Pentateuch.

The first category, Hebrew *tsara'at,* is variously translated as "leprous" (NRSV), "ritually unclean skin disease" (REB), or "eruption" (NJPS). The characteristics of this skin ailment are described in Lev. 13–14, and seem to be most like diseases such as psoriasis, acute acne, or vitiligo. The term probably encompassed a variety of skin diseases. In any case, the affliction was not Hansen's disease (popularly called "leprosy" in the modern world); this disease was not known in the Middle East in OT times. The more extended presentation in Leviticus specifies both observation periods of fourteen days and guidelines for evaluation of cases. The ceremonial or religious nature of the uncleanness is emphasized by the responsibility of the priest for examining persons and declaring them clean or unclean.

The second category, translated "discharge," refers in this context to any irregular discharge from the genitals. In the case of females, anything beyond the usual period of menstruation is meant (Lev. 15:25). As is clear from the more elaborate form of this regulation in Lev. 15, even indirect contact with such a person by touching personal effects such as bedding or clothing or saddles or pottery was regarded as contaminating and presumably to be avoided if at all possible.

The third category, contact with a corpse, is developed in detail in Num. 19 (see below). There the regulations focus on decontamination and there is no reference to being "put outside the camp."

Medically it may be reasonable to explain each of these regulations based on some understanding of contagious disease. Yet it is important to recognize that Israel's own rationale focuses on holiness. The community must not be contaminated because it is the place of God's dwelling. In these texts there is no statement that the contaminating condition is caused by the deity; nonetheless, the person afflicted is cut off both from human community and by implication from the presence of God.

Awareness of the religious as well as the human isolation of such an existence lends new power to NT stories of Jesus' healing of lepers (Luke 5:12ff.; Matt. 8:1-4) and of the woman with a discharge of blood (Mark 5:25-34; Luke 8:43-48). Christian communities across the globe continue to exclude various groups or individuals whom they consider to be "unclean," although the categories of exclusion today are more often related to social circumstances than to physical illness. Jesus' willingness to touch the "unclean" offers an inclusionary challenge to such exclusionary habits of the churches. So also Jesus' positive response to the woman who took the initiative to touch him (Mark 5:25-34; Luke 8:43-48) challenges the church to attend to the voices of those marginalized groups and persons ("outside the camp") calling for their own inclusion in the life of the community. (See Hisako Kinukawa, "The Story of the Hemorrhaging Woman [Mark 5:25-34] Read from a Japanese Feminist Context.")

5:5-10   This regulation deals with offenses among persons, in which one person takes property belonging to another. Again, additional details are offered in Lev. 6:1-7. Although one person has harmed another, the offense is regarded as equally against God (Num. 5:6). The provision for an atonement offering (v. 8) reinforces this theme. It is also reinforced by the requirement that restitution must be made without exception; if neither the wronged person nor any next of kin is available when the perpetrator confesses, restitution is made to the priest (v. 8). The law seems also intended to clarify that in cases when no next of kin is available any such donation belongs to the priest rather than to others (vv. 9-10). This tradition, so easily passed over, is notable for its practical uniting of the themes of love of God and love of neighbor. Offenses are not neatly divided into those against other people and those against the deity; to the contrary, offenses against neighbor are explicitly treated as offenses against God. Justice in the community and right worship of God cannot be separated; repentance and confession and even restitution involve both realms at once.

5:11-31   A long and complex regulation describes the procedure to be undertaken if a man suspects his wife of marital infidelity. Here the legislation promulgated focuses on men and men's rights and prerogatives. This is in contrast to the two preceding regulations where men and women are specifically treated in an equal way. Underlying this text is Israel's assumption that any sexual activity outside marriage is an offense against a man only. If a man has intercourse with an unmarried woman, her father is the offended party; if a man has intercourse with a married woman, her husband is the offended party. If the husband of a married woman has intercourse outside that marriage relationship, there is no provision for the wife to claim damages; only the father or husband of the other woman has been offended. Additionally, divorce could be initiated only by the husband, not by the wife, and the accepted grounds for divorce were adultery or incest. It could be supposed that this ritual is designed to prevent harm to women by protecting them from their husbands' suspicions. The tone of the text, however, suggests an androcentric focus in which men are given a ritual means of obtaining evidence to support their suspicions about their wives' behavior.

Verses 12-15a are constructed in the classic "if . . . then" structure of case law in the ancient Near East. The protasis or "if" clause states the circumstances of the case; the apodosis or "then" clause states what is to be done. Since the protasis here involves suspicion, the apodosis is stated in terms of a procedure for investigation rather than a specific punishment. In effect the apodosis continues through the subsequent description of the required ritual.

Although the goal of the ritual is to resolve cases of suspicion, the writer has constructed the "if" clause so that its dominant tone presumes the guilt of the suspected woman. Only in v. 14b does the possibility of the woman's innocence finally arise. A husband may bring his wife to the priest for testing not only if he has substantive grounds for suspicion but also if he simply is overcome by jealousy. The assumption of the woman's guilt is even more pronounced in the summarizing conclusion of the law (vv. 29-31), where there is no reference to her possible innocence. Although some commentators suggest that the woman agrees to the procedure to prove her innocence and thus to avoid divorce, there is no indication in the text that the woman has any choice about undergoing this ritual. If divorce is involved at all, it seems more likely that the text presupposes the necessity of evidence of infidelity as a basis for divorce and provides a ritual means of getting the necessary evidence. The disheveling of the woman's hair (v. 18) is usually taken as a sign of uncleanness, shaming, or mourning. This and the form of the oath (stating only the negative outcome; vv. 21-22) may be further indications that the text tends toward presuming the guilt of the woman.

The description of the procedure (vv. 15b-26) is complex. In its present literary form each stage of the action is first stated briefly, then an accompanying act is described. The main act of that stage is then stated in more detail (see Tikva Frymer-Kensky, "The Strange Case of the Suspected *Sotah*"). Once this pattern is recognized, the broad outline of the ritual may be followed in continuous sequence. The husband brings his wife to the priest with a specially prepared grain offering (v. 15). The priest brings her into the presence of God, prepares the ritual potion of water and dirt, and dishevels her hair. He has her take an oath while she holds the grain offering and he holds the potion (vv. 16-22). Then the priest writes out the previously spoken words and adds the ink to the potion (v. 23). In some translations it appears that in vv. 24-26 the woman drinks the potion both before and after the priest presents her offering at the altar; but v. 24 is to be understood as the heading for the next step that is specified in detail in vv. 25-26. All three components — the verbal oath, the potion to be drunk, and the offering — are integrated into a single ritual.

Some scholars (e.g., Baruch A. Levine, *Numbers 1–20,* 200, 212) use the word "magical" with regard to the potion; others (e.g., Timothy R. Ashley, *The Book of Numbers,* 124) reject this term on the grounds that the ritual involves God at every point. In any case, the text states that the potion itself "causes" the physical effects in the unfaithful woman (v. 27), and this aspect of the text must be taken seriously. Special water (the exact meaning of "holy" water, v. 17, is unclear) and special dirt (from the floor of the sanctuary), combined with ink from a written curse, are to produce a medically significant result in a guilty woman. Although modern heirs of the enlightenment and so-called scientific method may look askance at such consequences, comparable rituals in which apparently nontoxic ingredients are used to produce physical changes are attested in many cultures from around the globe. Belief in the efficacy of the potion as part of the full ritual is an important component. This is no more improbable than is belief in the efficacy of oath-taking or in the meaningfulness of bringing an offering before the deity.

Verses 27-28 describe the two possible outcomes of drinking the potion that will reveal the guilt or innocence of the woman. The precise meaning of the Hebrew phrases describing the possible outcomes of drinking the potion is not known; all theories about the medical conditions involved must at present be regarded as speculative. Some (e.g., Levine, 192-212) have argued that the results distinguish between miscarriage and continued pregnancy; but this approach assumes that only pregnancy would be cause for a husband's suspicions or jealousy. (Indeed, some early rabbis expressed concern that if the woman were pregnant the drinking of the potion could be construed as inducing abortion.) Other interpreters suppose that the contrast is between infertility and fertility in the future. Such an interpretation offers a broader context that seems warranted by general allusions to suspicion in vv. 13-14. This future-oriented interpretation, however, leaves the husband and the community without an immediate and definitive answer to his accusation. Again, the immediacy of the "guilty" result compared to the vague and future-oriented possible "innocent" outcome (on either theory) suggests a tacit assumption in the text that the woman is guilty.

The summation of this law, like the summation of most such laws, reiterates the main theme (vv. 29-30). In this case, however, a postscript is added in v. 31: "The man shall be free from iniquity." Since the verse continues that the woman "shall bear her iniquity," it has been suggested that "the man" in this context is the one with whom she has committed adultery. The difficulty, of course, is that the whole procedure is based on the absence of evidence. It is possible that the author of v. 31 supposes that the husband, or the community, knows who the guilty man must be; but this is nowhere stated. It is more likely, therefore, that "the man" here, as throughout the protasis, refers to the husband. Again, the guilt of the woman is presumed, so that the accuser is innocent of a false charge. In the absence of contrary evidence, it seems reasonable to interpret this verse more broadly: the husband is to be held innocent whatever the outcome, since this procedure exists for his sake so that he can find out the truth.

To some readers this text may seem an archaic relic of a bygone culture; to others it may resonate with procedures for settling marriage disputes familiar in their own contemporary communities. The question Christians must face is whether the biblical witness as a whole supports the imbalance of power between husband and wife in their marriage that is presumed here and in Israelite law generally. This text is to be classified with many other case laws of ancient Israel that are not applicable as direct rules for our own time. Thus this text does not offer a method appropriate to today for handling male jealousy. But the text does offer us a window into women's fear. It is not consistent with a Christian view of human flourishing that women should continue to live in the fear of false accusation that such a law must surely have produced. Yet women still do live in such fear. Fear of private beating or public humiliation by a wrongly jealous husband are common, not rare, conditions for women in our own time. In many cultures and in many individual marriages, fear of being seen speaking to another man or fear of misinterpretation of any sort of public behavior continue to haunt women's lives. The fear is caused by traditional male attitudes, and also by some continuing cultural assumptions about the inferiority of women. These assumptions are inconsistent with the biblical testimony of the first creation account, where both women and men are created fully in the image of God, and both are blessed by God (Gen. 1:27-28). Overall, the Bible calls Christians to love, mutuality, and trust in human relationships generally, and most especially in marriage. By these standards, attitudes and customs that lead to fear within marriage, whether in this ancient law or in contemporary families, must be judged incompatible with God's will for human life.

CHAPTER 6

6:1-21 Regulations are introduced concerning persons who make special vows as "nazirites." These are ordinary Israelites who set themselves apart to God, apparently for a period of time specified in their initial vow (Num. 6:5). As in 5:1-4 and 5-10, the nazirite regulation is explicitly for women as well as for men (6:2). The basic requirements of this vow are twofold: abstinence from any grape product and also from strong drink (the Hebrew word may mean "beer"), and refraining from cutting of hair (vv. 3-5). The familiarity of this latter requirement is indicated by the use of the Hebrew term *nazir* to designate an unpruned vine in Lev. 25:5.

Because those under a nazirite vow are "holy to the LORD," they must not allow themselves to become contaminated by contact with a corpse during the period of the vow (Num. 6:6). The strictness of this requirement is severe: no exception is made even in case of death of immediate family members (v. 7). Comparison to Lev. 21:1-4, 11 shows that this purity requirement is more strict than that for ordinary priests and is comparable to the requirement for the high priest.

Emergency purification procedures for cases of accidental contact with a corpse are given in Num. 6:9-12. The usual seven-day period of uncleanness applies (see ch. 19). Then the head is shaved in a special ritual and three sacrifices are to be presented at the sanctuary. The portion of the vowed time served up to the accidental contamination does not count; the full vow must be served from its beginning. The severity of the penalties and the value of the sacrifices required (especially a male year-old lamb) probably helped to insure that nazirites were careful to avoid such

40

contamination if at all possible. Underlying this regulation is the priestly conception that guilt requiring atonement can result even from such accidental violations of the requirements for purity (6:11). Both the holiness of the deity and the seriousness of the nazirite vow are emphasized by these emergency rituals.

The regulation for the conclusion of the period of nazirite service (vv. 13-20) further signifies the seriousness of this vow. Many offerings are required, representing the major categories of sacrifice and offerings known from ancient practice. Animals are provided for a burnt offering (also translated "whole" or "holocaust"; see Lev. 1), a sin offering (see Lev. 4), and an offering of well-being (also translated "shared" or "peace"; see Lev. 3). Additionally, a grain offering and a drink offering are brought (see Num. 15:1-16), with several kinds of specially prepared baked products used for an "elevation" offering. Based on the Mishnah, scholars believe this last offering was held high and carried in a sort of procession in the sanctuary. (Probably it was not "waved" to and fro, as the earlier English translation "wave" offering suggested.) The postscript to the summation of the law (6:21) suggests that the specified offerings represent the minimal amount expected. During these sacrificial rituals at the sanctuary marking the conclusion of the period of vowed nazirite lifestyle, the nazirite's head is shaved and the hair (grown throughout the duration of the vow) is burned in the fire for the sacrifice of well-being (v. 18). This ceremony reinforces the centrality of the requirement of unshorn hair.

The tradition of the nazirite vow is known from two narrative sources in addition to this legislative text. In both cases the circumstances are quite different from those presumed in Num. 6. The boy Samuel, born to an Ephraimite family, is dedicated "as a nazirite" by his mother Hannah for lifelong service (1 Sam. 1:22, 28, following the Qumran scroll version of 1 Samuel). The many subsequent stories about Samuel make no further reference, however, to conditions peculiar to nazirite vows. A second example of a nazirite is Samson. In this case, the angel of the LORD informs Samson's mother in advance that he is to be "a nazirite to God from birth" and that his hair shall never be cut (Judg. 13:5; cf. 16:17). Although Samson's hair is prominent in one part of the story, the only reference to abstinence from grape products and strong drink is in the angel's instruction to his mother for the duration of her pregnancy. Beyond these two stories of nazirites from birth, the principal additional OT evidence for this custom is the reference by the prophet Amos to nazirites and the efforts of the unfaithful people to undermine their vows by causing them to drink wine (Amos 2:11-12).

The tensions and inconsistencies between the regulation of Num. 6 and these other OT texts have occasioned a long scholarly debate. Some have viewed a lifelong dedication to the nazirite life as an early Israelite practice, with Num. 6 representing a late development of limited term vows. Others view the two options as existing side by side at least for part of Israel's history; still others have suggested that the idea of a lifelong nazirite is a literary embellishment of the Samson and Samuel stories but was never generally recognized in Israel.

Not only these historical queries, but many other potential points of interest for modern readers are left unanswered by the text. Why did people undertake such vows? How long did they typically last? (Thirty days seems to have been suggested in post-biblical Judaism, but nothing is known for the Israelite period.) What was the proportion of women to men? How were they regarded by the community? Were the shorn heads of women or men publicly exposed after the concluding rites? Quite possibly the answers to such questions changed over the many centuries of Israel's history. Such unanswered questions are reminders of the meagerness of our knowledge of the culture of ancient Israel.

Although these and other questions remain unanswerable, and although the text does not provide a direct explanation of the purpose of the nazirite vow, the regulations themselves and the other texts about nazirites suggest that such persons were to be regarded as especially close to God because of their vow. Throughout Christian tradition, many forms of short or longer term abstinence from ordinary practices have been associated with seeking a special relationship to God. One may think of the desert monks of the early centuries or commitments to periods of fasting by individual Christians. Isaiah 58 suggests that God seeks commitment to justice even more than public displays of personal piety; but this is not to deny the role of self-discipline for the sake of faithfulness in the practices of believers. The biblical nazirite tradition invites us to respect rather than disregard the disciplines of abstinence we encounter among Christian traditions differing from our own.

6:22-27 The words of a priestly benediction (in Christian circles usually called the "Aaronic benediction") appear abruptly, apparently not attached to the surrounding context. These words are usually regarded as those used by Aaron when he blessed the people at the conclusion of the investiture and dedication of the Aaronic priesthood (Lev. 9:22). Why the words have been so far displaced from this setting is not clear, although it may be noted that both Lev. 8–9 and Num. 7 are associated with the dedication of the tabernacle recorded in Exod. 40.

In 1986 archaeologists working in a burial site in the Hinnom Valley area of Jerusalem discovered two pieces of women's jewelry with portions of this benediction engraved upon them. Experts estimate that the amulets were made within the few decades preceding or following 600 B.C.E. The inscription provides rare extrabiblical testimony to the importance of a liturgical expression from the Bible in the lives of everyday Israelites. Scholars continue to consider how the shorter version of the benediction found on the jewelry relates to the longer biblical version, but all agree upon the beauty and artistic symmetry of the full biblical expression of the benediction.

As elsewhere throughout the Pentateuch, words of instruction to Aaron or the priests are given by God through Moses (Num. 18 is the significant exception). Even this benediction, a hallmark of the priestly responsibility, follows the standard pattern. It is the priests who are to pronounce the blessing, but 6:27 makes clear that it is God who does the actual blessing. Thus the pronouncing of these words is not to be understood as magical, as though the priests had power to withhold God's blessing by refusing to speak the words.

The blessing itself is composed of three lines (vv. 24, 25, 26), each incorporating the name of God, Yahweh (NRSV "the LORD"). The lines in Hebrew are of increasing length, whether one counts by words, by total consonants, or by syllables. The Hebrew phrases include much alliteration and repetition that is obscured in most English translations.

Blessing is the overarching category within this theologically dense benediction. This can be seen from the initial position of the word "bless" in the prayer itself (v. 24) and in the use of this verb for the speaking of the priests (v. 23) as they recite the prayer. Blessing in Hebrew tradition has to do with God's working for the good of all creation, and especially for human beings. Through divine blessing, the possibility of human flourishing is brought about. God's blessing provides the underlying and sustaining conditions for a full and satisfying earthly existence. Thus Israel understands blessing not just in some abstracted spiritual sense, and not just as a personal benefit. Offspring, land, possessions, and health are among the concrete expressions of God's blessing. Thus blessing involves physical well-being and access to adequate material resources; it is also communal, in that it is best expressed when such well-being and resources are available to all, not just to a few. The OT concept of blessing focuses upon the ongoing providence of God more than on special acts of divine intervention.

God "keeps" the Israelite community primarily by protecting it from danger, an ongoing guarding that provides the environment in which the positive features of blessing may flourish. This theme is well expressed in Ps. 121, where forms of the word "keep" occur no less than six times.

The "shining" or "lifted" face of God is a sign of divine favor; the first expression calls to mind the shining of Moses' face as he left the presence of God (Exod. 34:29-33). Although Israel recognized danger in "seeing" the face of God (Gen. 32:30; Exod. 33:20), the face of God is directed toward the people for their benefit. Psalm 80:3, 7, 19 associates the light of God's face especially with deliverance from enemies, as does Ps. 31:16. Thus the Aaronic blessing here could be construed by its hearers as a petition for continuing protection (keeping) in times of well-being or as a prayer for restoration in times of distress.

God's being "gracious" (grace) in the OT has to do with the receiving of undeserved gifts from God. These gifts include material blessing, freeing from enemies, and especially forgiveness of sins. The term appears frequently in liturgical and narrative settings (e.g., Exod. 33:19; 34:6; Ps. 27:7; 31:9; 2 Kgs. 13:23; Jonah 4:2), and the concept is foundational for Israel's self-understanding long before the NT era. In the Old Epic tradition, divine graciousness is included in the full liturgical title of God revealed to Moses at Mt. Sinai (Exod. 33–34), where it is explicitly related to divine forgiveness. In the era of the Monarchy God's graciousness is cited as the basis for the continued existence of the people despite their failings (2 Kgs. 13:23). And the prophet Jonah cites the old liturgical title from Exodus to explain why he had not wanted to prophesy in Nineveh: Jonah knew that God was so gracious that even the hated enemy Ninevites would receive divine forgiveness! For Christians, God's work in Jesus Christ to which the NT bears witness is the seal and confirmation of God's will to forgive all peoples that is already clearly visible in many parts of the OT.

The words of the blessing conclude with the invoking of God's "peace" *(shalom)*. Although in the narrower sense this term sometimes refers to the absence of war, and thus may seem connected to the invocation of God's "keeping" from danger, the term *shalom* has a much broader meaning of all that is involved in human well-being. Thus it is appropriate and significant that this noun appears last in the Hebrew of this benediction, providing an all-encompassing term corresponding to the all-encompassing opening word in the Hebrew, the verb "bless." In its beginning and its ending, this benediction is about the providence of God. Used at the conclusion of worship, it provides a bridge between the people's gathering to praise God and their dispersing to life in the world. The God who is praised in worship is committed to uphold the fragile daily existence of the worshipping community.

CHAPTER 7

Numbers 7–9 take the reader back in time to the day of the completion and consecration of the tabernacle. The completion of the sanctuary is described in Exod. 40; its consecration with oil is reported in Lev. 8 in connection with the consecration of the Aaronic priesthood. Exodus 40:17 gives the first day of the first month of the second year as the date of setting up the tabernacle. Numbers 1:1 dates the command to take a census one month later, on the first day of the second month of the second year. Numbers 9:1, however, refers again to the first month of the second year, and the subject matter of chs. 7–8 is explicitly connected to the setting up of the sanctuary (7:1). Thus the events described in Num. 7–9 appear to be set one month earlier than the beginning of the book. It is only with Num. 10:11 that the story line returns to the chronological sequence established in 1:1. Chapter 7 opens the "flashback" by describing presentations of offerings by the tribal leaders on the occasion of the completion of the tabernacle.

7:1-9 The leaders first present as a group six wagons and twelve oxen, presumably two oxen to pull each wagon. These are to be used by the Gershonite and Merarite divisions of the Levites for transporting the tabernacle, as described in ch. 4; since the Kohathites were assigned the most sacred objects, ones equipped with poles for hand-carrying, they do not receive oxen or wagons. Tensions in the chronology are present: this distribution of the wagons and oxen presumes the information of ch. 4 about the duties of these three Levitical divisions; yet, as explained above, 7:1 dates this event to an earlier time than the instructions of ch. 4.

46

7:10-88   The bulk of this long chapter enumerates the offerings presented by each tribal leader at the time of the anointing of the altar. The names of the tribal leaders are the same as those assigned in 1:5-16 to assist Moses with the initial census. They are mentioned again as tribal leaders in the instructions for camp locations in 2:3-31. The order of the list here follows the encampment sequence of ch. 2. All twelve tribal leaders make identical offerings. The offerings are made on twelve successive days; 7:88 indicates that the twelve days followed the actual anointing of the altar.

To some modern readers the text may seem needlessly repetitious, with its twelvefold identical reiteration of the offering list. In its form it most likely reflects the manner of record keeping for donations of the ancient temple. The list is easily charted, and such tabular records are known from Mesopotamian and Canaanite documents unearthed by archaeologists.

In its adaptation to a literary context, several purposes are achieved by the recordlike style of this section. The importance of each tribe and the equality of their responsibility for sacred things and gifts to God are lifted up. The weight and solemnity of the ceremony of presentation are set forth in the detailed recording of each day's offering; the reader is led to picture each leader coming forward with his tribe's dedicatory gifts, and to imagine the ceremonial recording of these gifts as they are presented. At the same time, the magnitude and value of the gifts themselves are highlighted by the daily summaries that precede the final totals in vv. 84-88. It is estimated that the silver plates weighed about 1.5 kg. each, the silver basins about 0.75 kg. each, and the gold dishes about 114-122 gm. each (see R. B. Y. Scott, "Weights and Measures of the Bible"). The animals total twenty-one per tribe, and are all mature or yearlings.

Additionally, the repetition emphasizes that the major categories of regular offerings are provided for: grain (see Lev. 2), burnt (see Lev. 1), sin (see Lev. 4), and well-being (see Lev. 3). Leviticus 4 indicates that the sin offering is to be made whenever an individual (v. 3) or the whole congregation (v. 13) commits an unintentional offense. This offering, however, was probably offered routinely at the beginning of tabernacle/temple rites, as preparation and as expiation for unknown offenses (Anson Rainey, "The Order of Sacrifices in Old Testament Ritual Texts").

7:89   The concluding verse of Num. 7 is cryptic, and its relation to its context is unclear. Some translators interpret the Hebrew to reflect a single occurrence, what happened at the end of the twelve days. Most, however, presume that this verse describes what regularly and repeatedly happened whenever Moses entered the tent of meeting. The absence of the name of God in the Hebrew, as well as the use of several pronouns without clear antecedents, further obscures the meaning. Most likely, as interpreted in the NRSV translation, the focus is on the voice of God and from where Moses hears it. "The Voice" comes from above the ark of the covenant, between the cherubim. (OT cherubim are composite animals with wings; they are not the winged human infants of later Christian art, nor are they angels, which in the OT are depicted as adult male figures without wings.) Although the cherubim mentioned here are small and part of the gold cover of the sacred ark (Exod. 25:17-22), in the Jerusalem temple there were large cherubim (whose wings touched the walls of the innermost part of the sanctuary; 1 Kgs. 6:23-28) with the ark kept below them (1 Kgs. 8:7). Israelite tradition understood Yahweh to be invisibly enthroned upon the cherubim, with the ark for a footstool (e.g., 2 Kgs. 19:15; 1 Sam. 4:4; Ps. 99).

Although this verse stands in isolation, its location here serves as a reminder of the dual function of the tent of meeting. Numbers 7–8 (and indeed much of Leviticus to Numbers up to this point) concentrate on sacrifices and the rituals of worship that were the responsibility of the institutional leadership of priests and Levites. Numbers 7:89 draws attention to the tent not as the place where the priests and Levites do their work, but rather as the place where Moses, the fountainhead of all prophecy, hears "The Voice" of God. The final form of the Pentateuch seeks throughout to balance the roles and importance of Moses and Aaron (see ch. 20); 7:89 in its setting is a part of this effort at balancing. The verse calls to mind God's promise to meet with Moses at the tent of meeting (Exod. 25:22), as well as an older tradition of God's speaking with Moses in a tent (remembered as being outside the

camp; Exod. 33:7-11). The sanctuary as the holiest place is thus
connected not only to routinized worship but also to the possibility of new revelation.

CHAPTER 8

8:1-4   As in Num. 3:2-4 and 4:5-14, this chapter is concerned mainly with the Levites (8:5ff) which opens with reference to a duty of the Aaronic priesthood. Here, however, the reason for introducing the instruction about the sanctuary lamps is not easily discernible. Specifications for construction of the stand and its lamps were given to Moses in Exod. 25:31-40, and the report of carrying out these instructions is given in Exod. 37:17-24. Exodus 25:37 states that the arrangement of the lamps should cast light toward the front. This detail is not mentioned in Exod. 37, which focuses on construction but not on setting up. Numbers 8:1-4 apparently seeks to reintroduce the arrangement commanded to Moses in Exod. 25 by further specific instruction through Moses to Aaron. As is typical of the Priestly tradition, the exact carrying out of God's command is noted. The report of correct placement of the lamps may be given here as part of the theme of bringing the sanctuary into service through the anointing and dedicatory sacrifices described in Num. 7.

The lamps and stand mentioned here form the menorah or branched lampstand. This feature became important in the later Jewish tradition of Hanukkah, the Feast of Dedication or Feast of Lights. This feast originally celebrated the purification and rededication of the temple after its pagan desecration; the story is recorded in the deuterocanonical book of 2 Maccabees. Scholars cannot reconstruct just how the festival came to focus on lights and to feature branched candlesticks in individual homes. However it happened, this celebration continues even today as a solemn yet joyous occasion in the life of the Jewish community. Its date of celebration, determined by the Jewish calendar, usually falls in early to mid-December.

8:5-22   Moses receives instructions for the consecration of the Levites to their sacral duties (vv. 5-19), and these instructions are carried out (vv. 20-22). The larger biblical treatment of Levites indicates that the rite is for males only, although the text does not specify this restriction. The ceremonial cleansing and the necessary offerings bear some resemblance to those undertaken for the consecration of Aaron and his sons (Lev. 8). The rites mentioned for the Levites, however, are less elaborate and omit the anointing with blood and oil and the vesting with garments described for the Aaronic priests.

The Levitical ordination rite involves two main parts. First there is bodily preparation, including shaving, washing the body, and washing the clothes. The association of each of these acts with cleansing and purification is known from other texts. All three are present together in Lev. 14:8-9, the rite for cleansing from skin disease. Washing of clothes and body appears also in Num. 19 concerning contact with a corpse, and shaving of a nazirite's head must be done after contact with a corpse (6:9) as well as at the end of the period of the nazirite vow. Washing of clothes was part of the preparation required of all Israel before God appeared to the people at Mt. Sinai (Exod. 19:10). The "water of purification" mentioned in Num. 8:7 suggests something more than ordinary bathing, however, and the exact expression appears only here in the Hebrew Bible. It may be related to the specially prepared water described in ch. 19. Whatever the background of this unique expression, context shows that the sprinkling of the water on the prospective Levite was intended to remove impurity.

The second part of the rite is the presentation of the Levites by Aaron at the sanctuary, with both a sin offering and a burnt offering. Like the first, this aspect of the ceremony is intended to make the Levites pure so that they may be close to the holy deity, fit to serve without danger of being destroyed by contact between the holy and the unclean. The consecrated Levites are understood to be both a gift to God (as an "elevation offering";

8:11, 13; see 6:20) and a gift from God to the Aaronic priests
(8:19). The theme of the substitution for the firstborn has appeared already in 3:40-43 (see commentary there).

The ceremony features laying on of hands: the hands of the
Israelites upon the Levites (8:10), and the hands of the Levites
upon the bulls they have brought for the sacrifices (v. 12). Again
this theme is one known from diverse sacral contexts in the OT
record. For examples of this, see 27:18, 23 and Deut. 34:9 (where
Moses' authority is transferred to Joshua); Lev. 3:2 and 4:4 (in
the context of kinds of sacrifice); and Lev. 24:14 (in the context
of a death penalty). Here it appears that the act of laying on hands
designates the Levites and the animals for the function to which
they are being dedicated. The general procedure for the burnt
offering outlined in Lev. 1 includes the laying of the donor's hand
on the animal so that it will be "acceptable in your behalf as
atonement for you" (Lev. 1:4). The service of the Levites is
explained here as "to make atonement for the Israelites" (Num.
8:19), a sort of living sacrifice. Laying on of hands continues as
part of ordination rites in most Christian traditions, but it is
generally done by the existing leaders, not by the people. Thus
its function differs, in that it serves to pass on and distribute
special authority, more like what Moses does for Joshua in Num.
27:18-23.

In their role of assisting Aaron and his sons, the Levites serve
as an additional buffer between God and the people. The idea of
zones of holiness within and around the sanctuary has already
been seen in the restriction that only the priests (not the Levites)
may touch or even look upon the ark and its appurtenances
(4:5-20; see Introduction). Here the Levites themselves are said
to protect the rest of the congregation against plague by taking
up duties that would bring the ordinary worshippers too danger-
ously close to the sanctuary (8:19). This role of the Levites has
been anticipated in 1:51-53, where their responsibility for "guard
duty" prevents divine wrath from falling upon the congregation.
Divine holiness in Israel's understanding requires that God be
approached with fear and awe, not in any casual manner.

8:23-26   A brief appendix to the consecration of the Levites specifies that they may serve from the age of twenty-five to the age of fifty. The first part of this regulation obviously disagrees with the regulation given in 4:3, 23, 30, where the age range for those "who qualify to do work relating to the tent of meeting" is from thirty years to fifty years. Here a different regulation, probably from a different era or reflecting different circumstances, has been preserved; the biblical tradition seems content to let the regulations lie side by side without comment. Scholarly explanations are nearly as numerous as the published commentaries. They include theories about periods of apprenticeship, about the need for greater maturity among the leaders, and about a scarcity of Levites or a need to limit their numbers in proportion to the priests. One or another of these theories may be historically correct, but in the absence of any textual clues, all must be regarded as speculative.

The previous problem is compounded because of broader uncertainties about the role of the Levites. The precise nature of the duties of the Levites "in attendance on Aaron and his sons" is not specified beyond standing guard and carrying the portable sanctuary as described in chs. 3–4 (see also ch. 18). But in the temple era there was no movable sanctuary. Even though contact with the most sacred objects was restricted to the priests, it is possible to imagine various sorts of help that a group not entitled to offer sacrifices themselves might have rendered during the ceremonies. The text neither specifies nor forbids such duties. Further, as explained in the Introduction, the overall history of the relationship between the priests and Levites is unclear; the picture of Levites assisting the priests is generally agreed upon for the Second Temple period, but even the existence of a separate class of Levites in the era of the First Temple is much debated.

CHAPTER 9

9:1-14 Instructions concerning the Passover are given, supplementing the Passover regulations that are set forth in Exod. 12. God's command to Moses (9:1) at the beginning of the second year establishes the requirement of an annual celebration that is implicit in the institution of the Passover as a "perpetual ordinance" in Exod. 12:24. The date and time specified in Num. 9:3a conform to the instructions of Exod. 12; the "statutes and regulations" mentioned in Num. 9:3b apparently also refer to Exod. 12. As is typical of Priestly material, the execution of God's command by the people is duly noted.

Numbers 9:6 introduces the specific problem of persons unclean because of contact with a dead body. (Note that this theme of contact with a corpse comes up not only here, but in chs. 6, 19, and 31.) Those contaminated ask Moses what is possible for them with regard to the Passover. Although they approach Moses "on that day" (of the Passover; the exact time sequence is not clear), they assume that they are unable to participate in the rite and express their dismay at this exclusion (9:7). Moses seeks God's instruction concerning their complaint, and the answer received forms additional legislation for a circumstance not previously envisioned. God's reply is intended as a permanent guideline, as seen by the inclusion of the phrase "or your descendants" (v. 10). This literary pattern of new legislation being introduced in response to a specific inquiry is found for other regulations in chs. 27 and 36; the pattern may give some indication of the actual process by which law developed over time in ancient Israel.

God's reply in 9:9-14 is not, however, restricted to the question presented by those who have touched a corpse. Those who have been "away on a journey" (v. 10) are also to follow the special regulation of observing the Passover one month later than usual. The details of vv. 11-12 beyond the date highlight main features of the celebration to emphasize that the observance should be identical in every respect except the date.

Additionally, a severe penalty is introduced for any person who is able to celebrate the Passover at the proper time but does not do so (v. 13). In v. 13 cleanness is a general condition; the possible causes of uncleanness are unstated and thus are not restricted to contact with a corpse. Hence the provision in v. 10 for a delayed Passover is implicitly expanded to cover other cases of ritual uncleanness.

The case of the resident alien (v. 14) who is to follow all the regulations is much farther removed from the opening question to Moses than even the rule about those on a journey, for here the regulation considers non-Israelites. A process of accretion appears to be at work, whereby further guidelines on the general topic of the Passover have simply been attached. Both the journey and the existence of resident aliens seem to presuppose a time far removed from the supposed wilderness context. Unlike vv. 10 and 13, v. 14 does not appear to supply information unavailable elsewhere in the tradition. Rather, like v. 12 it repeats in briefer form the regulation of Exod. 12:48-49, omitting the explicit requirement of circumcision. Perhaps its presence here is explained by its proximity both here and in Exod. 12 to the regulation against breaking bones of the Passover animal.

Although this regulation appears to apply to men only, the matter is not completely self-evident. There is no explicit reference to women. The concept of the Passover as "presenting" an "offering," which is an act normally restricted to males in Israelite worship, suggests that the problem lies in the domain of males as heads of household. According to the Exodus regulations, however, Passover is a family by family rite in which it is presumed that everyone participates in the eating of the roasted lamb. It is possible that the ritual uncleanness of a female household member might be cause for delaying the celebration. Later rabbinic tradition considered both menstruation (see Lev. 15:19-23) and the period of uncleanness after childbirth (see Lev. 12:1-5) as conditions precluding participation in Passover rites (Milgrom, *Numbers*, 68).

The precise meaning of the punishment for disobedience is not certain, but to be "cut off from the people" was surely construed as a severe penalty. The expression is not infrequent as a judgment in Priestly material, appearing for example concerning the sabbath (Exod. 31:12-14), absence of circumcision (Gen. 17:14), various sexual offenses (Lev. 18:20ff.), and improper eating of sacrificial offerings (Lev. 19:8). Probably the earliest meaning of the penalty was some form of banishment, but by the time of the Mishnah Jewish tradition construed it as "death at the hands of heaven" (cited in Levine, *Numbers 1–20*, 466).

9:15-23   These verses appear to be an elaboration of the same theme found at the very end of the story of construction of the tabernacle in Exod. 40:34-38. The paragraph establishes the presence of God in the sanctuary, symbolized by cloud and fire. It then explains how the Israelites knew when to strike camp, dismantle the tabernacle, and move on in their wilderness journey. In Exod. 40 this knowledge is based strictly on the movement of the cloud; here in Numbers the theme of God's command is introduced as well (Num. 9:18, 20, 23). The Hebrew word for command used here is literally "mouth," suggesting an oral instruction through Moses (v. 23b), not simply indirect instruction by the moving of the cloud. Although fire is mentioned in both texts as the nighttime appearance of the cloud, the fire is not specifically mentioned in the signals for moving or encamping. The Numbers text emphasizes both the obedience of the community to this signal and the variable length of the various encampments on the journey.

The grammar of the Hebrew both here and in Exod. 40 represents what would typically happen, rather than describing a one-time event. The passage looks to the immediate future when the journey from Sinai to Canaan begins. Within the overall structure of the Pentateuch, these verses are surely intended as a resumption of Exod. 40, chronologically as well as theologically. Only the making of trumpets is still to be described (Num. 10:1-10) before the first description of the lifting of the cloud and the moving of the camp (10:11). These trumpets were to be blown to signal breaking camp (10:2). Despite the distinctive beginning of 1:1 (see commentary), the texts of Exod. 40:34-38 and Num. 9:15-23 form a literary bracket. All of the legislation of Leviticus and of Numbers up to this point appears within this bracket.

The glory of God, manifest to Israel in cloud and fire, filled the tabernacle at its completion. This glorious brightness, known in later Jewish tradition as the Shekinah, indicated the presence of God. It provided a way of speaking of God's immanent presence in the sphere of human life while still preserving the mystery of God's otherness and transcendence. Israel also described this paradox of the immanence and transcendence of God in the language of darkness; references to brightness and to darkness are juxtaposed in Ps. 18:11-12 and in 1 Kgs. 8:10-13 (the climax of the dedication of Solomon's temple).

The glorious presence in the tabernacle provided the possibility for God to be in the midst of Israel even after the people departed from Mt. Sinai. God who appeared at Sinai (Exod. 19) was not restricted to that mountain, but would be present with the people in the movable sacred tent and would lead them on their journey. The concept that a god could be present with the people wherever they moved was not commonplace in the ancient world; many believed that gods were especially associated with certain sanctuaries bearing the name of the god, and thus with certain geographical regions. It seems that even in the era of the Monarchy many Israelites held this view about their God. In the time of the Babylonian exile (after the fall of the monarchy and the end of the Israelite nation-state) it was therefore especially important to underline the idea that God was not restricted geographically and could be with the people even in a strange land, even in adverse circumstances. The Priestly writer's description of the tabernacle, with God's accompanying presence through the wilderness, is a key biblical source for this idea.

Moses' communication from God similarly moved from the Sinai mountaintop to the tabernacle, once it had been dedicated. But a core of sacred revelation, especially cultic regulation, was remembered as basic and as belonging to the era before the

57

departure from the region of Sinai. This core included, among much else, establishment of the system of offerings and sacrifices and the ordination of leadership for institutional worship. Thus Leviticus as a whole is presented as God's words to Moses "from the tent of meeting" (Lev. 1:1), but the tent is still located in the wilderness of Sinai. Likewise, the opening part of Numbers is located in the "wilderness of Sinai" (Num. 1:1) where the people had first arrived before the Sinai theophany (Exod. 19:1).

Eventually Jewish tradition came to regard all the Pentateuch (narrative as well as legislation) as equally sacred and foundational tradition. Even so, legislative texts in the remainder of Numbers are structurally supplementary (although not therefore secondary) to the Sinai legislation. In a similar way, Deuteronomy is presented as a "review" of previous legislation, even though it includes new and different material.

CHAPTER 10

10:1-10   The opening verses record divine instruction for one last aspect of preparation for an orderly march through the wilderness. Two silver trumpets are to be made, and instructions are given for their use by the priests to summon the leaders or the entire congregation, to break camp, to go to war, and to celebrate festival occasions. Since one use of the trumpets is to signal breaking camp, these verses are appropriately positioned before the first breaking of camp (Num. 10:11ff.). Nevertheless, the paragraph seems almost an afterthought. The usual formula of Moses' obedience to the divine command is missing; the text does not report the making of these trumpets. Furthermore, they do not figure in the following description of breaking camp; indeed, they are only mentioned once more in the wilderness narratives, when they are sent into battle (31:6). The more frequent reference to this kind of trumpet is in 1-2 Chronicles. There such trumpets are mentioned more than ten times in connection with festivals of rejoicing (e.g., 1 Chr. 16:6; 2 Chr. 5:12; 15:14), indicating their importance for later temple tradition.

JOURNEY FROM
SINAI TO MOAB
(10:11–21:35)

CHAPTER 10 (CONTINUED)

The remainder of Num. 10 introduces the next major phase of Israel's life. The book of Exodus records the people's departure from Egypt and then their travel to the wilderness of Sinai (Exod. 15:22–19:1). The remainder of Exodus, all of Leviticus, and the book of Numbers up to this point record what took place either in that wilderness area or more specifically at Mt. Sinai itself within that area. Now the people have received all of the basic divine instruction and are ready to set out on their journey toward the Promised Land. The subsequent chapters will reveal both that the journey will be long delayed and that additional instruction must be given by God.

In this section of Num. 10 we are introduced to three aspects of the guidance of the people through the wilderness: the cloud (vv. 11-28), a human guide familiar with the wilderness (vv. 29-32), and the ark of the covenant (vv. 33-36).

10:11-28   With the lifting of the cloud as their signal, the Israelites make their first move away from the wilderness of Sinai (vv. 11-12). This movement from the wilderness of Sinai to the wilderness of Paran is the first specific example of the guidance by the cloud that was anticipated in detail in 9:15-23. The exact location and direction of the move are not certain, especially since the location of Mt. Sinai itself is disputed. Third century C.E. tradition located the mountain in the south of the Sinai Peninsula, but there are no older records. If this traditional location is accurate, then the people moved generally north-northeast. The date of departure given in 10:11 is nineteen days after the date of 1:1. (The material in 7:1ff. looks back to a time one month earlier than the date of 1:1; see commentary at 7:1 and 9:1.)

Numbers 10:13-28 summarizes the "order of march" (v. 28) for the wilderness journeying. The focus is on proper care for the sacred tabernacle and its "holy things" (contents). The description of the line of march, the names of the leaders, and the duties of the Levites follow the order and information given in chs. 2–4. As in the earlier chapters, the description combines sacral and military language. Judah, the tribe of the later Davidic monarchy, again has the preeminent position. Once the tabernacle has been taken down, the Gershonites and Merarites assigned to carry the tabernacle proceed ahead, and the tabernacle is re-erected and ready to receive the sacred objects by the time the Kohathites arrive carrying the contents (10:17, 21). Surprisingly, no specific mention is made of the place of the priests themselves in the line of march. It should also be noted (although this is not surprising) that no attention is given to the place of women and children in the procession.

10:29-32   These verses raise the possibility of a human guide in the wilderness. Here material often attributed to the Old Epic (JE) tradition (see Introduction) reappears in the Pentateuch for the first time since Exod. 34. Priestly material and its point of view will continue to dominate the book of Numbers, but more incorporation of traditions from a different style and perspective will be apparent in chs. 10–24.

The exact relationship of Hobab to Moses is uncertain. The Hebrew grammar of 10:29 allows either Hobab or Reuel the title of father-in-law. In Judg. 4:11 Hobab is clearly named as Moses' father-in-law. Other passages give other names for Moses' father-in-law. In Exod. 2:18 he is called Reuel; in Exod. 18:1 his name is reported to be Jethro (cf. Exod. 3:1; 4:18). The inconsistencies in naming probably reflect a combination of differing ancient memories and partial harmonizations of tradition, which the final editors of the Pentateuch did not feel at liberty to change. The story fragment ends abruptly after Moses for a second time urges Hobab to accompany the people. Although we are not told whether Hobab returned to his kindred or joined the traveling

Israelites, Judg. 4:11 suggests that Hobab's descendants did enter the land along with the Israelites.

In Judg. 4:11 Hobab is identified as a Kenite; here Hobab/Reuel is a Midianite. Jethro is clearly remembered as a Midianite in the Exodus references. Israel's relationship to the Midianites and Kenites was significant historically, although its exact form is shrouded in the folkloric character of many of the references. Even the exact relationship between the Midianities and Kenites cannot be reconstructed with certainty. Taken together, however, the various passages mentioning Moses' in-laws point to the significance of those relatives for Israel's faith and their participation in Yahweh worship. Exodus 18:9 reports that Jethro "rejoiced for all the good that the LORD had done to Israel" and worshipped the God whom he recognized as "greater than all gods." Here Moses urges Hobab to participate in this same "good" in the future, "for the LORD has promised good to Israel." Many scholars specializing in the history of Israel's religion connect the beginnings of worship of God under the name Yahweh with contact with the Midianites. This theory notes especially Moses' association with a Midianite priest at the time of the burning bush theophany when the name Yahweh was revealed to Moses (see Exod. 3:1, 13-15). Other traditions, however, especially in Num. 25 and 31, suggest a very negative relationship between the Israelites and the Midianites; these negative traditions are generally associated with the Priestly writing, rather than with the Old Epic contribution to the tradition.

The potential value of a Midianite as an effective wilderness guide is supported by the tradition of Midianite shepherds (Exod. 3). Such shepherds would have moved about extensively in their search for pasturage and thus would be familiar with the desert region and its water supplies. Yet Hobab's answer to Moses' request to serve as guide is conspicuously absent from the story. This omission is probably to be understood theologically. Numbers 9:15-23 has established that the people move and set up camp expressly at God's command, and the cloud over the tabernacle indicates the new place of encampment (9:17). Thus no human guide is necessary from the perspective of the tabernacle tradition. Also, in the immediately following verses, Num. 10:33-

34 (probably Old Epic tradition), it is the role of the ark of the covenant to find the next camping place. The preservation of Moses' request, however, suggests a tradition that included human guidance by those familiar with the wilderness. The themes of divine and human guidance are not in principle incompatible; but the narrator wants to emphasize that God's guidance is indispensable.

10:33-36 These verses offer yet a third perspective on guidance in the wilderness. Although the mention of the cloud (v. 34) is reminiscent of vv. 11-12 where the cloud moves from over the tabernacle, here it is the ark of the covenant that is pictured as leading the people and seeking their next stopping place. The words attributed to Moses (vv. 35-36) appear to be the first lines of two ancient songs. Like 9:15-23, these words recall a frequently repeated occurrence. In this case, the occurrence that is recalled is the singing when the ark was moved. The lines are placed into the narrative here on the occasion of the departure of the ark from the wilderness of Sinai where the ark was originally made and sanctified.

In these poetic lines God is pictured as a divine warrior, invisibly enthroned over the ark (see commentary on 7:89; also 2 Sam. 6:2). Although the literary context created by Num. 10:33 is concerned with divine travel guidance, the poetry itself focuses more on the military function of the ark as representing divine leadership in going out to battle (v. 35; cf. Ps. 68:1) and in returning home after battle (Num. 10:36). This understanding of the ark is attested in narratives from the period before the ark was placed inside the temple in Jerusalem during Solomon's reign. The ark as representative of God's leading in battle appears first in 14:44, where Israel's defeat is attributed to the absence of the ark and of God from the battle scene. The same concept is also found in the so-called "ark narrative" of 1 Sam. 4–6. These traditions understand the deity invisibly enthroned upon the ark as "the LORD of hosts," a frequent biblical expression that refers to God as leader of the heavenly army. It is this army that fights along with and gives victory to Israel's earthly military forces; no victory is possible for Israel apart from the LORD of hosts.

The ark also played a role in various religious processions, representing the presence of God with the worshipping community. Tradition recalled that when the priests carrying the ark stood in the Jordan River, the river waters were cut off (Josh. 4), a sign to the nations of God's power (Josh. 4:24). Probably premonarchical Israelites reenacted this memory in a religious procession from the sanctuary of Gilgal near the bank of the Jordan. Psalm 24 suggests a procession of the ark through the city of Jerusalem (or at least through the temple precincts) in the period of the Monarchy. The fate of the ark after the destruction of the First Temple in 587 B.C.E. is not known.

Like the tabernacle, the ark tradition addresses the question of how and where the presence of God may be known and experienced. The traditions about the ark emphasized its mobility (even though during the Monarchy it was housed inside the temple), and thus that God was not confined to one place. Even the physical design of the ark suggested its mobility, since it was equipped with carrying poles (Exod. 25:12-15; cf. 1 Kgs. 8:7-8). The theological presentation of the tabernacle and ark in Exodus and Numbers combines the idea of mobility with the idea that the sanctuary is the meeting place between heaven and earth where God is sure to be present. According to some texts the glory/presence/cloud of God is permanently present in the tabernacle (see, e.g., Exod. 40:38); yet according to other texts the cloud comes only when God speaks to Moses (see Exod. 33:9ff.), or it is removed from the tabernacle when journeying time comes (Exod. 40:36-37). The very existence of the ark of the covenant in Israel's midst symbolizes the presence of the invisible God. Yet the mobility of the ark reinforces the idea that God is on the move, not locked into one place (not even the tabernacle or the temple).

The importance of this concept that the God who is both transcendent and immanent is not tied to a single sacred space cannot be underestimated (see also commentary on Num. 9:15-23). This idea provided a basis for the people exiled to Babylon to comprehend that their God had not abandoned them. It allowed for the development of synagogue worship and diaspora Judaism. Christian tradition carries forward the same theme in its witness to God's presence "wherever two or three are gathered."

CHAPTER 11

Chapter 11 deals with food in the wilderness and problems of the designated leaders of the people. Aspects of these themes appear also in Exod. 16–18, and scholars have long noted the overlapping of Exodus and Numbers here. The problems concerning food and leadership are typical of many situations where people are on the move and under stress. These understandably arise as soon as the Israelites leave the structured life of Egypt. The appearance of these themes both immediately preceding and immediately following the Sinai account creates a literary bracket of complaints and disputes surrounding the narrative of the Sinai revelation. This literary arrangement suggests something of the complexity of transmission of these traditions as explained in the Introduction. Theologically, this larger literary structure sets apart the holiness of Mt. Sinai and the sanctity of the time spent there from the more mundane concerns with which Israel struggles in the space and time surrounding the Sinai revelation.

Numbers 11 intertwines a story of the people's desire for meat with a story of Moses' frustration about his task as leader. Although the story is unified by its general narrative structure and by the theme of complaining, its two aspects raise different questions for theological reflection.

11:1-3 The chapter opens with a brief story that explains why a certain place is named Taberah, which means "burning." The vagueness of the story about the complaint of the people suggests that the place name is a central feature here, although scholars cannot identify its exact location. The nature of the "fire of the LORD" also cannot be determined, although the theme of divine fire as an expression of God's judgment is known from other passages (e.g., 26:10; 2 Kgs. 1:12), and it is a regularly appearing image for the wrath of God in both Psalms and prophetic literature. An important feature of this story is the reinforcement of Moses' role as intercessor for the people when they are in distress. Moses is the one who has a special relationship with God; it is to Moses' prayers that God will particularly listen and respond. This picture of Moses as the intercessor par excellence began to be developed in Exodus (especially Exod. 32), and it will be seen again elsewhere in Numbers, especially in Num. 14. The theme of the intercessor here in 11:1-3 also provides a dramatic backdrop for Moses' own complaining in the subsequent paragraphs of the chapter.

11:4-9   Manna as described in vv. 7-9 was once thought to be the fruit of a species of lichen plant. That species is not known today in the Sinai Peninsula. What the Bible describes as manna is now thought to be the excretion of scale lice that suck large quantities of sap from tamarisk trees. In the desert air the sweetish droplets quickly dry to sticky solids ranging from the size of a pinhead up to the size of a pea. It has been estimated that a person could collect up to one kilogram per day during the peak season in June. As with the quail (below, vv. 31-34), an understanding of the natural phenomenon does not "explain" the biblical story; it only provides a background in nature. The manna from the tamarisks is found only in a limited area of the Sinai, and in quantities too small to sustain a large number of people (G. Ernest Wright, *Biblical Archaeology,* 64-65). In a culture where neither beet nor cane sugar was known, any sweet treat would be memorable, especially one in a desert area where honey was not available.

Such explanations of the sustenance in the wilderness are of interest to many modern readers. It is important to recognize, however, that the biblical narrator does not focus on such naturalistic or scientific questions. Rather, the narrator is interested in the food as divine gift, evidence of God's power to provide and symbolic of the wilderness journey (cf. Josh. 5:12, which reports that the manna ceased on the day when the Israelites first ate of the produce of the land west of the Jordan River).

To appreciate the wrongness of the people's complaint about the manna in Num. 11:6, and thus to understand why God becomes so angry, it is necessary to read this story in connection with the manna narrative of Exod. 16. There the people complain of having nothing at all to eat, remembering when they ate their "fill of bread" in Egypt (Exod. 16:3). In response, God provides manna for all Israel as daily provision. As described poetically in Ps. 78:23-24, God "commanded the skies above, and opened the doors of heaven; he rained down on them manna to eat, and gave them the grain of heaven. Mortals ate of the bread of angels; he sent them food in abundance." Exodus 16 also emphasizes that each person was able to gather just the right amount so that household by household the people had enough for daily bread. None had too much, and none had too little. The manna had to be consumed on a daily basis and could not be kept overnight. An exception was made on the day before the sabbath. At this time, everyone miraculously gathered a double portion, half of which could be kept, so that there was no gathering to be done on the sabbath. When some disobeyed and searched, they could find no manna.

The Jewish theologian Martin Buber spoke of "miracle" in the Hebrew scriptures not as an event contrary to our usual expectation of the natural order, but rather as an experience of "abiding astonishment" (*Moses: The Revelation and the Covenant*, 75-76). The miracle of the manna is not just its existence. It is not just that there was enough to feed everyone over a long period of time. It is much more that each one had enough for daily bread; no one had too little, and no one had too much. The apostle Paul apparently thought that this perfect distribution might have been possible because the Israelites pooled the manna collected and then divided it up (2 Cor. 8:13-15); but the OT story does not give any detail of how the necessary distribution took place.

The text of Exod. 16 does not explain why some gathered more manna and some gathered less (Exod. 16:17). Surely some Israelites were physically stronger and some were weaker. Probably some were zealous, hoping to get a larger share, while others were apathetic, not supposing that this odd food supply would make much difference to their survival. Perhaps some were compulsive workers at any assigned task, while others were just lazy, trying to get away with the minimum required to meet Moses' instructions. What is clear is that weakness, apathy, and laziness did not prevent God from supplying daily bread, and that strength, zeal, and compulsiveness did not yield more than daily bread. God's gracious provision was bestowed according to need, not according to merit or motive.

With this story of Exod. 16 as background, the people's complaint in Num. 11:6 can be seen as a new phase of their discontent. They say that the manna is inadequate for sustenance and that they are bored with it ("there is nothing at all but this manna to look at"). Now they are no longer complaining of empty stomachs. Rather, they object to the inadequacy of what God has provided. Their thoughts turn fondly to life in Egypt, where there was variety of food. In their longing they seem to forget the harsh conditions that accompanied their servitude under the pharaoh and his overseers. Perhaps their longing is typical of people under great stress who often forget the negative aspects of any alternative situation to which they may dream of retreating. Similarly, the dream of the future, the land promised by God toward which the people are moving, has fallen out of Israel's thinking. Their only focus is on their present misery.

Rabbinic tradition draws special attention to the phrase "for nothing" (v. 5), i.e., "free of charge." The meaning may be simply that the pharaoh fed the slaves so that they would have strength to work. At another level, however, the manna of the wilderness is associated with the giving of the commandments and the need for obedience (Exod. 16:4; cf. Deut. 8:3). As Michael Walzer points out, slavery does provide "freedom" from certain choices that cannot be made by enslaved persons. Freedom from slavery, on the other hand, involves "servitude" to a level of obligation and responsibility, in this case to the commandments of God (*Exodus and Revolution,* 52-53). In contrast to the people's complaints about their slavery in the opening chapters of Exodus, the wilderness traditions are filled with stories of this same people complaining about the consequences of their freedom.

71

11:10-15   Both Moses and the LORD react negatively to the people's weeping complaint. Moses' prayer to God (Num. 11:11-15) gives vent to his frustration and outrage at the situation in which he finds himself. Unlike the people (who complain but do not address anyone in particular), Moses addresses his complaint directly to the deity. Moses insists that God has not favored him, indeed has done the opposite, by setting him as leader over this people. In v. 12 Moses compares the formation of the people to a mother who "conceives" and "brings forth"; he insists that he has not brought forth this people and that therefore he should not bear the responsibility of a wet-nurse to feed and care for them. Moses insists that the burden is too heavy (v. 14). He suggests that God must either change the situation or put him to death so that he can escape from his misery.

Several features of this prayer deserve attention. First, its composition produces a powerful literary effect through the use of contrasting pronouns. Moses' resentment toward God is apparent in this text; this can be seen clearly by reading the text aloud with special emphasis on the words that occur in first and second person. Everything is God's fault, as Moses sees it. Again a narrative in Exodus provides background for understanding the Numbers account, particularly for interpreting Moses' negative attitude here. In the story of Moses' call (Exod. 3–4) he is portrayed as a man who does not want to take on the responsibility of leadership. He appears as a man who suggests that the people will not accept his leadership. When that objection is overcome, Moses next complains that he is inadequate to the task. The intent of the Exodus narrative is to show that Moses is definitely the leader whom God has chosen, that no substitute will do. In Num. 11 he again protests his inadequacy to the task. Now he protests on the basis of the actual behavior of the people rather than on imagined future difficulties. Yet the Moses portrayed here still does not express any expectation that God can or will rectify the situation. He is content merely to give strong expression to his displeasure.

Second, in comparing his role to that of a mother, Moses' rhetorical intent is to attribute this role to God. Although God is never addressed directly as mother in the OT (and only very rarely as father), in various places God is compared to a mother who conceives and brings forth children. Deuteronomy 32:18 chastises the Israelites for forgetting "the Rock that bore you; . . . the God who gave you birth." God says, "I will cry out like a woman in labor, I will gasp and pant" (Isa. 42:14). Such occurrences, although relatively rare, make an important contribution to the diversity of biblical imagery for God. God is compared to aspects of both genders, female as well as male, not just to male biology and roles. Such diversity is a part of the biblical basis for the ancient and continuing theological claim of the church that God is neither male nor female but is beyond male and female.

It is less clear whether or not the reference in Moses' prayer to the nurse carrying the sucking child should also be related to God. The word for nurse here is grammatically masculine in the Hebrew, apparently because Moses is picturing himself in the role. The reference to a "sucking" child suggests that the image is of a wet-nurse, and the context of a discussion about food and feeding seems to confirm this meaning. Why is the comparison to a wet-nurse introduced, rather than just continuing with the image of the *mother* carrying a sucking child? The answer may lie in the difference between the initial formation and the continuing leadership of the people. Moses is clear that he did not "conceive" or "bring forth" Israel; God has done that. There is, however, a need for some kind of human leadership for this people brought forth by God. It may be this need that presses the next stage of imagery toward the wet-nurse who assists the birth mother and provides nourishment. Moses reminds God that he never wanted this leadership obligation in the first place. Whether the image is of mother or of wet-nurse, the responsibility is to provide food and generally to care for the helpless infant. Moses does not want the burden of this helpless and complaining people.

Third, the two prongs of Moses' specific complaint (Num. 11:13 and 14) set the stage for the response of God and the remainder of the chapter. Up to this point the narrative has been simply about sustenance, and Moses' despair over the demand for meat continues that theme. But his inability to "carry" (like a nurse) and his insistence on the impossibility of his task overall indicate that more must be done. In the context of the final form of the whole Pentateuch, this complaint about the burden of leadership may seem puzzling. Exodus 18 reports that Moses had appointed able leaders of subdivisions of the people to "bear the burden with [him]" (Exod. 18:22). In the history of the composition of the Pentateuch, it is likely that the two stories about leadership represent different traditions about how assistance for Moses was established, even as there are different traditions about the meat in Exod. 16 and Num. 11. Since the leaders in Exod. 18 are assigned to judge simple cases, while the role of those in Num. 11 has to do with prophecy (see below), the two stories are not finally contradictory but rather are aimed at explaining the origin of different features of Israel's life as a community.

11:16-23   God's reply to Moses addresses both Moses' own complaint about the burden of leadership (vv. 16-17) and the complaint of the people about their food supply (vv. 18-20). The instruction for establishing shared leadership is stated in a matter-of-fact tone, with the intended outcome that Moses will not bear the burden alone. God does not appear displeased with Moses' complaint. By contrast, however, the tone and content of God's response to the people's complaint dramatically express the anger of God mentioned in v. 10. Meat will be provided in excess, until it seems loathsome to the people. The true significance of their complaint about food is stated clearly: "you have rejected the LORD who is among you" (v. 20). The criticism of God's miraculously provided manna and the lament over departing Egypt are not idle complaining; they constitute apostasy.

This motif of the people's complaining and God's response appears repeatedly in the traditions of Exodus and Numbers. Numbers 14:22 mentions a round number of ten such incidents, although the text does not record ten instances preceding that chapter. Including later incidents, as many as fourteen such individual stories are recorded (Exod. 5:15–6:1; 13:17–14:31; 15:22-25; 16:1-36; 17:1-7; 32–34; Num. 11:1-3; 11:4-34; 12; 13–14; 16:1–17:11; 20:2-13; 21:4-9; 25). A general pattern of divine response to the complaints can be discerned. In the time before God establishes the covenant with the people at Mt. Sinai,

God simply responds to their expressed needs. Beginning with the "golden calf" incident (Exod. 32) and continuing with this Numbers story and onward, however, God expresses displeasure and imposes judgment upon their complaints (see Num. 11:33), even though the substance of the complaint (here, meat) may be answered by some divine provision.

Many biblical psalms are full of complaining to God. It is often said that such psalms bear witness that people should express their deepest feelings frankly before God. Is there a difference between these wilderness narratives and the prayers of the Psalter? Do the Exodus and Numbers narratives serve as a warning against such frankness? Clues to these questions may be found by considering the setting in life and the literary genres of the Psalms on the one hand and these narratives of complaint on the other hand.

In the Psalter, the genre is one of prayer directed to God in situations of anguish. Even the query "why have you forsaken me?" (Ps. 22) is predicated upon the petitioner's presuming and desiring a relationship with God. Most Psalms of this type insist that the petitioner is faithful and innocent, and emphasize the petitioner's intent to serve God faithfully, even while asking why disaster has come. A smaller number are penitential psalms expressing the petitioner's repentance for wrongdoing and asking for relief from the resulting judgment (e.g., Ps. 38, 51).

By contrast, the people in Num. 11 never address God directly. They complain among themselves and are overheard by God. Furthermore, their longing for Egypt is taken as a symbol of their lack of belief in the power of God. It shows their lack of trust that God is among them, and their wish that the Sinai covenant had never come into being.

In sum, the lamenting psalmists protest (as did Moses) directly to God, presuming the goodness and favor of God even as they are mystified and frustrated by the negative turn of their fortunes. The wilderness Israelites do not call upon God. They do not take their relationship to God seriously. They do not take seriously God's declaration of love and care for them, which is implied in the deliverance from Egypt. The psalmists struggle with God; the wilderness Israelites ignore God. The contrast provides clues for the faithful who seek to trace out the fuzzy line between questioning God and rejecting God.

11:24-30   The sharing of God's spirit among seventy elders takes place at the sacred tent (the place of God's presence), in answer to Moses' complaint to God. The number seventy is a traditional one, appearing often in the Bible (e.g., Exod. 1:5; 24:1; Judg. 8:30; Luke 10:1), and may indicate a large number rather than an exact count. Here Moses is presented as the fountainhead of prophecy, since the elders prophesy after they receive a portion of God's spirit that was upon Moses. Scholars have puzzled over the lack of further prophecy by those receiving the Spirit (Num. 11:25c). Perhaps this note distinguishes the role of all other persons from the special role of Moses during the wilderness period. God speaks through Moses in a unique way, as will be made clear in the story recorded in ch. 12.

The bulk of this section concerns two men, Eldad and Medad. These two were registered among the seventy. For some reason, they had not proceeded to the tent, which in this tradition is pictured as being outside the camp, not in its center as in ch. 2. The spirit came upon them nevertheless, as among those registered, and they also prophesied. Moses' assistant Joshua (who is a key figure in the biblical book of Joshua) urged Moses to stop their prophesying, but Moses rebuked Joshua, not the two elders: "Would that all the LORD's people were prophets . . . !" This brief but important story sets forth dramatically the tensions between institutionalized and noninstitutionalized leadership in a religious community. Joshua is worried either that Eldad and Medad did not receive the Spirit in the prescribed mode (at the tent), or else that they were still prophesying after the others had ceased. Moses' response lends legitimacy and power to prophesying that takes place outside standardized channels.

From the time of Samuel on to postexilic times, Israel's political and religious leadership struggled with the "problem" of prophets whom they could not control. This leadership had difficulties with prophets who were not part of the establishment and who criticized the establishment and its institutionalized prophetic leadership. Through the centuries the church also has continued to struggle with how to recognize the voice of God among those who have not been properly ordained to leadership, especially among those who challenge existing structures and teachings. The story of the elders and of Eldad and Medad serves to remind every generation that God's Spirit among the people should be welcomed. The story reinforces the idea that God's Spirit is not restricted by human rituals or institutions (cf. Mark 9:38-40).

11:31-34 The people's complaint (Num. 11:4-6) is now answered in accordance with God's word to Moses (vv. 18-20). An overabundance of quail is carried in from the sea by a wind from the LORD.

The conclusion of the story about the people's craving for meat maintains the tension between divine provision and divine judgment seen earlier in the chapter (vv. 10, 18-20). The people need not search for the quail; they are abundant for all. Yet a plague from God kills many, and the place is remembered by the name "Graves of Craving," Kibroth-hattaavah. Like Taberah (v. 3), this wilderness site cannot be located with certainty.

Like the manna, the appearance of many quail has been given scientific explanation that provides general credibility to such a source of sustenance in the Sinai Peninsula. In the months of September and October, annual migrations of quail fly from Europe toward Arabia and Africa. After flying across the Mediterranean Sea many of them are reported to flop exhausted on the Sinai shore area. Thus the narrative's claim that large numbers of birds could readily be picked up from the ground seems possible within the realm of nature. Nevertheless, this natural phenomenon does not fit exactly with the biblical account. Exodus 13:17 indicates that the escaping Israelites did not follow the coastal route (the "way of the land of the Philistines"). Rather, they traveled far inland into the Sinai Peninsula (Wright, 60-65). In the same way, the plague (Num. 11:33) that follows might be explained as a consequence of eating spoiled meat or diseased birds, or even as a reaction to consuming a large quantity of meat when the digestive system was not accustomed to animal protein.

As was pointed out in the commentary on vv. 4-9, however, the biblical narrative is focused on religious rather than scientific questions. The narrator's attention is fixed upon divine power as the source of what happens. Indeed, ancient Israel would have been puzzled by the effort of many modern cultures to distinguish between "natural" and "supernatural" events. From Israel's perspective, all events were rooted in the power of God; some events might be more unusual than others, but none took place apart from God. The primary question for ancient Near Eastern cultures generally was not "How did this happen?" but rather "Who (which deity) caused this to happen?" For Israel, of course, the answer is clear: Yahweh is the source both of judgment and of blessing.

CHAPTER 12

12:1-4 The theme of leadership in addition to Moses was introduced in ch. 11 with Moses' desire for assistance. Here that theme takes a new turn with the complaint of Miriam and Aaron against Moses. Moses' brother Aaron is already a familiar figure from earlier chapters of Numbers. He is remembered as the first high priest and fountainhead of the line of the Aaronic priesthood. Miriam has not been mentioned since Exod. 15:20-21, where she is identified as Aaron's sister (and therefore by implication also Moses' sister). According to Exod. 15, she led the Israelite women in singing after the deliverance from Pharaoh's army at the Red Sea. Tradition assumes that Miriam was the older sister who watched over the baby Moses in his floating basket (Exod. 2:4, 7-8), although she is not named in that story. The three are remembered together in one later text as leaders sent by God (Mic. 6:4).

Miriam and Aaron voice their complaint (Num. 12:1-2) and "suddenly" (v. 4) the voice of God is heard summoning the three to the tent of meeting. The Hebrew adverb suggests a startling intrusion and hints that God is displeased, although this is not made explicit until v. 9. Verse 3 serves as a parenthesis, explaining to the reader that the humble Moses would not take up his own cause against the accusation, so that it is God's responsibility to defend Moses.

The complaint made against Moses is twofold: that he has married a Cushite, and that he claims exclusive authority as God's spokesperson. Although the center section of the chapter focuses solely on the second complaint, the first complaint also raises significant questions.

Who was the Cushite wife? Where was Cush? What objection did Aaron and Miriam have to this wife? She is mentioned only here, so hypotheses have been developed by inference from a variety of other passages. There is no certainty and little agreement about the answers to these questions, although the questions are interlocked. Exodus 3–4 reports Moses' marriage to a woman named Zipporah, a daughter of a priest of Midian. Was the Cushite wife this same Zipporah or a different woman? From the earliest rabbinic tradition scholars have debated this question. If the Cushite wife was Zipporah, then there should be some connection between Midianites and Cushites. Habakkuk 3:7 seems to suggest such a connection (if "Cushan" is the same as "Cush"). The tradition records many connections between Moses and Midianites; the Midianites are generally viewed positively in Old Epic stories and negatively in the Priestly strand of pentateuchal tradition. If Cush was a subgroup of Midian, then the criticism of Moses' wife in Num. 12 may reflect a conflict between a pro-Moses group and a pro-Aaron group during the era of the Monarchy (Cross, *Canaanite Myth and Hebrew Epic*, 203-4). The objection to Moses' wife on this analysis is simply that she is of Midianite background. The analysis is plausible from a history-of-religions point of view. It focuses, however, upon a dispute that must be reconstructed from scattered hints and is no longer in the forefront of the narrative.

Other biblical references place Cush either to the north of Israel (north Syria or Mesopotamia; Gen. 2:13 as interpreted by many scholars) or in the far south in the area of Ethiopia (Gen. 10:6; 2 Kgs. 19:9; some scholars regard Gen. 2:13 as also a reference to Ethiopia). Since connections of either of these locations with Midian are less probable, many scholars conclude that Moses' Cushite wife is not Zipporah. They follow the Septuagint tradition in assuming that this wife is Ethiopian, therefore black in skin color. The punishment of Miriam, in which her skin turns to an unclean white color (Num. 12:10), is then understood as a sort of "poetic justice." Why would Aaron and Miriam object to a black woman as Moses' wife? Some scholars have argued for a traditional prejudice against black skin; but recent scholarship suggests that this is a modern European prejudice, not known in the biblical period (see Cain Hope Felder, *Troubling Biblical Waters,* ch. 3). Others propose that dark skin may have been highly regarded and that this marriage would have created jealousy by giving Moses even higher status in the community than he already had (Randall C. Bailey, "Beyond Identification"). Still another approach is to suppose that skin color was not the central issue at all, but that rivalry between Miriam (and Aaron) and the new sister-in-law was the root of the complaint (Renita J. Weems, *Just a Sister Away,* 72ff.).

The identity of the Cushite wife and the reason for complaint against her cannot finally be resolved. It is important, however, to note the significance of this story in Christian circles where the legitimacy of interracial marriages has been debated. Both in the United States and South Africa (and no doubt elsewhere as well), the tradition of marriage between Moses and a black woman has played a powerful role in the discussion of this topic. On the assumption that the complaint of Miriam and Aaron was based in racial prejudice, God's rejection of their complaint has been used to show that the biblical testimony supports the permissibility of interracial marriage. If, however, the ancient world did not recognize racial groupings or know racial prejudice as we experience it today, the connection to the modern debate cannot be made so directly. Nonetheless, the very absence from the Bible of prejudice based on racial groupings, as well as the Bible's positive understanding that all people are created equally in the image of God, offers a strong biblical witness to the permissibility of such marriages.

12:5-9   God addresses Miriam and Aaron in a speech intended to establish the uniqueness of Moses' role and to rebuke their challenge against Moses. The central part of the speech (vv. 6-8) is given in the form of poetry. Although the poetry is very difficult to translate and interpret in detail, Moses is clearly validated as one whose contact with God differs materially from that of all (other) prophets. By implication, Aaron as priest does not receive such communication from God; other prophets such as Miriam (Exod. 15:20) or those receiving a portion of the Spirit (Num. 11) receive a lesser form of communication.

Such ordinary prophets receive communication from God in visions or dreams (12:6). These means of prophetic communication are known from references scattered throughout the OT. 1 Samuel 9:9 speaks of "seers" (of visions) as another name for prophets. Dreams are mentioned alongside visions and prophesying in Joel 2:28. Jeremiah 23:25-28 and Deut. 13:2-5 suggest that genuine prophets have dreams given by God, but that the community must beware of false claims to such revelations. By contrast to revelation through dream or vision, Moses actually "beholds the form" of God and receives God's word "face to face" (Num. 12:8). Given Israel's tradition that looking upon God's face results in death, this is a powerful claim for Moses' uniqueness, even if the expression "face to face" is taken figuratively to express direct contact between Moses and God. Although Exod. 33:11 also mentions God speaking to Moses "face to face," another tradition in that same chapter (vv. 17-23) reports that even Moses was able to see only the "back" of God. Despite such ambivalence in the overall tradition, the goal of Num. 12 is to highlight Moses' intimate association with the transcendent God. This establishes his unique position even in relation to his brother and sister.

12:10-16 After God departs in anger, Aaron discovers that Miriam has turned white from a skin disease (not Hansen's disease; see commentary on 5:1-4). He immediately intercedes for her to Moses, who in turn intercedes with God. The phrasing of Aaron's plea, "do not punish us," suggests he was motivated at least in part by fear that the same fate would befall him as had happened already to his sister. Shutting out a woman whose father "spit in her face" is not known elsewhere in biblical tradition; but spitting as an indication of shame or disgrace is alluded to in Deut. 25:9; Isa. 50:6; and Job 30:10. A period of seven days' quarantine and examination for healing in cases of skin disease is prescribed in Lev. 13. Quarantine outside the camp is required in Num. 5:1-4, and is reflected for a city context in the story of 2 Kgs. 7:3-10.

Why is only Miriam punished, not Aaron? Some have argued that Aaron was not originally a part of the story. In support of this idea it may be noted that Miriam is mentioned before Aaron in Num. 12:1. It should also be noted that her punishment may be viewed as "poetic justice" for complaining about a black woman (see above). Also, the theme of prophetic status relates more properly to Miriam than to Aaron. On the other hand, it is exceedingly difficult to reconstruct a Miriam-only narrative from the extant text of ch. 12. The final version of the story, whatever its prehistory, distinguishes between the fates of Aaron and Miriam.

A second possible reason for Aaron's escape from punishment relates to his role as the first high priest. Purity regulations for the high priest were even more stringent than for the general priesthood (Lev. 21:10-15; cf. also commentary on Num. 16:36-40 and 19:1-10). No priest who had a skin disease could eat of the priests' food (Lev. 22:4). The idea that the famous Aaron could have been so afflicted would be extremely difficult for the bearers of this tradition to accept, however much they may have especially honored Moses. Aaron is pictured as praying for deliverance in anticipation of being afflicted like Miriam ("do not punish *us*," Num. 12:11). He thus admits his guilt but does not need to go through the ritual quarantine and purification period. This explanation, focusing on Aaron as high priest, fits well with the protective treatment of Aaron in the narrative of the golden calf (Exod. 32). In that story Aaron is not punished, does not repent, and is not even explicitly declared guilty, even though he led the people in making an idol. One goal of the final form of the pentateuchal tradition is to balance the roles of Moses and Aaron as precursors of the prophetic and priestly traditions (see commentary on Num. 20). It seems to be part of this strategy to present narratives that show Aaron's weakness, yet to avoid picturing him as the object of divine judgment.

A third possibility for explaining the punishment of Miriam alone rests on the suggestion that Miriam had developed a considerable following in later times, probably among groups of women. While there is no direct evidence for such a Miriam movement, if such a movement did exist this story may represent an effort to criticize and discredit it while upholding the male leadership of both Aaron and Moses.

Whatever the interpretation of the dissimilar treatment of Miriam and Aaron in this narrative, the inequity of severe punishment for one and no punishment for the other remains a fact of the text. All three proposals suggest in different ways the androcentrism of the culture that preserved the story. Either Miriam is fully to blame, or she is not accorded the special protection offered to a male religious leader, or her followers are wrong for elevating her to a position comparable to male leaders. As in many cultures today and throughout history, the consequences of challenging authority fall far more heavily upon the woman than upon the man.

CHAPTER 13

13:1-24   Numbers 13–14 relate the initial and disastrous attempt of the people to enter the land promised them by God. At God's command, twelve men are chosen to spy out the land. None of the individuals named are mentioned among those representing their tribes in the early chapters of Numbers. Caleb from Judah and Joshua (Hoshea) from Ephraim play a key role in this story and in the history of the next generation who finally enter the land.

Moses sends out the spies with a list of categories for them to assess. The categories are about equally divided between military intelligence and the desirability of the land for habitation. The brief report of their travel (13:21-24) indicates that they spied out the entire territory of what eventually became Israel in the time of David and Solomon, from the southern Negeb northward into modern Syria (Lebo-hamath, v. 21).

13:25-33   The spies return with their report to the leaders and the people. According to vv. 25-29 they are agreed about the marvelous productivity of the land, which they describe as "flowing with milk and honey" (v. 27); and all are agreed about the strength of the inhabitants and the strong fortification of their towns. They are divided, however, as to the appropriate course of action. Caleb proposes to take the land at once. The others consider the task impossible and reinforce their conclusion by describing the Israelites as like grasshoppers compared to the huge people who live in that land "that devours its inhabitants" (v. 32). The image of a devouring land may be intended to dramatize the power of the human forces living in Canaan, or it may be a reversal of the earlier claim about the fruitfulness of the area. In any case, the recommendation against proceeding to the land is evident.

CHAPTER 14

14:1-10 As anticipated already in 13:30, the congregation focuses on the reports of danger and fear. They complain to Moses and Aaron (still not directly addressing God; see commentary on ch. 11). They wish they had already died, and then begin conspiring to replace Moses and return to Egypt. The expression of fear for wives and children (14:3) reveals the storytellers' focus on the men of the community as those weeping, complaining, and conspiring. This perspective fits with the use of sacral language of "congregation" and "assembly" as the worshipping community in which the place of women is usually invisible in the tradition (Judith Plaskow, *Standing Again at Sinai*, 2-10). Moses and Aaron are rightly dismayed, and Caleb, with Joshua now joining him, speaks again of the goodness of the land. They urge the people not to rebel against God; victory depends upon God, not upon the strength of the opposition. But the appeal is to no avail; the people threaten to kill them. At this juncture God intervenes, as the glory of the LORD appears at the sacred tent.

14:11-38 This section presents a lengthy consideration of the consequences of the people's "rebellion" (v. 9). The broad outline of the section is as follows:

vv. 11-12   God proposes to disinherit (and strike with pestilence) the people and create a new nation out of Moses;

vv. 13-19   Moses urges God to relent and forgive the people;

vv. 20-25   God agrees to forgive them but says nevertheless that none will see the Promised Land except Caleb;

vv. 26-35   God speaks again, addressing both Moses and Aaron. The theme of death in the wilderness is made explicit but is modified to preserve alive Joshua and the second generation along with Caleb. The forty-year wilderness sojourn is announced;

vv. 36-38   the ten spies who brought the bad report die by plague.

There are many smaller and larger tensions that suggest layering of tradition in this theologically pivotal story of the wilderness era. One of these tensions is the inconsistency in mentioning Caleb alone or mentioning Joshua alongside Caleb. Another is the variation in address between "Moses" and "Moses and Aaron." Also, there is an inconsistency even after Moses' intercession between the pronouncement of death for all the people and the saving of the second generation. Before discussing the important theological themes present here, a few comments about the probable development of this story within the community of Israel may help to explain some of these tensions.

The narrative is part of a series of stories continuing in Josh. 14:6-15; 15:13-19 and Judg. 1:10-15 that explain how Caleb's family came to be in possession of Hebron. This question was no doubt of great interest to the later community. King David, who was a descendant of the clan of Judah to which Caleb belonged, was first crowned king in Hebron. This happened some time before he captured Jerusalem and set up headquarters there (2 Sam. 5:1-5). Many scholars who have studied these traditions closely believe that they reflect an ancient historical kernel about a group under Caleb's leadership. According to these scholars, this group entered Canaan from the direction of Kadesh in the south, not across the Jordan River. This Calebite group captured and occupied Hebron. It seems likely that this group was not originally Israelite, but became a part of Israel once the community

was being established in the land west of the Jordan. The books
of Joshua and Judges make clear that the process of the formation
of Israel was very complicated and that many groups who were
already in the land at the time of Joshua were incorporated into
Israel. In Num. 14 an ancient story about this Calebite group
has been adapted to an all-Israelite perspective. Caleb still has a
key role, but the all-Israelite leader Joshua is now a major figure
as well. Similarly, the idea that the second generation enters
Canaan together from the east is incorporated into the received
version of the story. As in the oral traditions of many cultures, a
local hero (Caleb) has been elevated to a national hero in this
process; but tensions in the story give clues to its earlier version.

The starting point for assessing the theological significance of
this story is the seriousness of the sin involved in the people's
refusal to claim God's promise and go up to the land. The key
sentence is in God's words of 14:11a, "How long will this people
despise me?" The verb "to despise" (Heb. *ni'ets*) appears again
in v. 23b: "none of those who despised me shall see [the land]."
This verb is used in the OT only when people are spurning God
or something sacred to God. "To despise" is thus a highly charged
religious term, and the action of the people is in fact a rejection
of their whole covenant relationship with God. In the wilderness
context, the rejection of the land is in itself symbolic of rejection
of the covenant. The goal of God's relationship with the people
from the moment of their departure from Egypt has been to
bring them to the land promised to their ancestors (Gen. 12:7).
To refuse to enter the land is to reject the goal of the relationship.
The people's lack of trust in God manifests itself in their proposal
to replace Moses with another leader and to go back to Egypt.
This behavior is aptly characterized by the key word "despise."
Despising, from a Hebrew perspective, is sin "with a high hand."
It is deliberate action, not inadvertent sin for which expiation
might be made; such deliberate sin inevitably has negative consequences. God may not give up on the people altogether, but
some form of judgment must result; life cannot simply continue
unchanged after the sin of "despising."

In fact God does not give up on the people altogether, and
the second theological theme to be considered is thus divine

forgiveness. The principal focus of the possibility for forgiveness, and the clue for the interpretation of the nature of God's forgiveness, is in the word that the NRSV translates as "steadfast love" (Num. 14:18, 19), Hebrew *hesed*. This word refers to the loyalty that an individual or group with power in a specific situation offers to the party in that relationship who is lacking in power. The use of the term *hesed* presumes a relationship between those involved, here God and Israel, so the covenant context is implied.

When *hesed* is spoken of in human relationships in the Hebrew Bible, it never has connotations of forgiveness; when the Bible speaks of God's *hesed*, however, forgiveness becomes a central feature. *Hesed* is help offered to a person or group in distress, essential assistance, usually help that no one else is in a position to offer. All these features of the word are present in God's forgiveness of Israel.

Divine forgiveness is especially associated with the phrase "abounding in steadfast love" (Hebrew *rab-hesed*) that appears here in an old liturgical formula (v. 18). Also occurring in many OT prayers to God, this phrase is used only with reference to God. In the covenant context God alone is in control and is free to act or not to act, to forgive or not to forgive. Moses' intercession is not a mechanical device by which God can be forced to respond favorably. Yet the phrase *rab-hesed* points to God's faithful commitment to the people, a commitment that goes far beyond any human standard. Moses' intercession is addressed to a God who forgives beyond human imagining. When Moses prays to God, "Forgive . . . according to the greatness of your steadfast love" (v. 19), his use of the term *hesed* concerns both God's attitude and God's action. In invoking *hesed* Moses asks God both to show a more faithful attitude than the people have a right to expect and to act to provide deliverance beyond their deserving by turning back from the judgment of disinheritance.

Immediately God announces forgiveness (v. 20) in response to Moses' plea. Yet in the same sentence, the same breath, God also announces punishment of the rebels. What kind of forgiveness is this? To answer this question it is essential to recognize that the content of God's forgiveness here is the nondestruction of the *people,* the very continuation of God's relationship to the *community* as God's community. It is the *hesed*-based decision not to create a new nation of Moses or anyone else, and not to disinherit this community because of its unfaithfulness. Christians sometimes become so accustomed to thinking of forgiveness in individual terms that it is difficult to recognize this continuation of relationship with the community as a sign of forgiveness. From an OT perspective, continuation of the covenant relationship with God is the basic good, the basic content of forgiveness. Such forgiveness is not abrogated or cheapened by a specific punishment meted out within that covenant context.

Preservation of the covenant with Israel is based in God's *hesed,* in the faithfulness that God freely maintains to the commitment God has made. Forgiveness is always a *surprising* act of sheer grace, to be received with joy and thanksgiving. Yet the final form of the Numbers story looks back even beyond the Sinai covenant to the tradition of God's promise sworn to Israel's ancestors (v. 23). Moses' prayer appealed to God's reputation among the nations (vv. 15-16) and to the Sinai covenant tradition of God's full liturgical name (v. 18; cf. the self-proclamation of God's name in Exod. 34:6-7). The Sinai tradition taken alone, however, was dependent upon Israel's obedience (Exod. 19:5); God might forgive many times, but there was always the possibility that forgiveness would be withheld the next time the people sinned. The final editing of this story probably took place during the time of exile in Babylon. This was a situation of despair when the nations were mocking the Israelites and their God (Ps. 137:1-3). A sense of abandonment had settled upon many of the exiles (Isa. 40:27). By looking to the unconditional promise given to Abraham (Num. 14:23; see Gen. 12:1-3; Isa. 51:1-3), God's response to Moses' prayer assures the Israelite community that God's *promised* steadfast love will not let them go. Whatever failure, whatever sin there may have been, the foundational promise to the community across the generations holds true, not only for the ancient wilderness generation, but for every generation, even those in Babylon (Katharine Doob Sakenfeld, "The Problem of Divine Forgiveness in Numbers 14").

Christians sometimes speak disparagingly of the wrathful God of the OT. There are many stories of divine judgment, to be sure. However, the more basic witness of the OT is to the overarching, undergirding, and unchangeable steadfast love of God for this people who are called to be a blessing to the nations (Gen. 12:3). The NT witness to God's love in Jesus Christ does not introduce a brand new theme; rather it confirms and amplifies a central tenet of the Hebrew Scriptures that is exemplified in Num. 14.

14:39-45 Moses reports to the people God's words of covenant faithfulness and of judgment, whereupon the people repent of their rebellion and propose to do what God originally wanted them to do. Moses insists that the time is no longer right and that their new effort to go to the land is further transgression. God's decree will not be reversed, and they cannot take the land without divine support. On the absence of the ark from the scene of battle (Num. 14:44), see the commentary on 10:35-36. The people attempt an incursion nonetheless and are immediately repulsed. Thus begins the long sojourn in the wilderness.

CHAPTER 15

Abruptly the narrative sequence of chs. 10–14 is interrupted by a miscellaneous series of cultic regulations, most (as in chs. 5 and 9) supplementing legislation prescribed earlier in Exodus or Leviticus.

15:1-16 The requirement of grain and drink offerings to accompany animal sacrifices that will be burned has appeared already in connection with the law of the nazirite (6:14-17). According to ch. 7 each tribal leader presented a grain offering along with his animal offering at the tabernacle dedication. (There an incense offering is mentioned, but no drink offering.) Leviticus 1–3 gives procedural instructions for certain animal offerings and grain offerings but does not connect the two. Numbers 15:1-16 now provides supplemental instructions. These specify that grain and drink offerings shall regularly accompany offerings by fire (v. 3). The exact requirements are given for these offerings in the separate cases of offering a lamb (vv. 4-5), a ram (vv. 6-7), or a bull (vv. 8-10). The quantity of the accompanying offerings increases in accordance with the value of the animal being offered. The stated requirements are specified to be amounts per animal, not per occasion (vv. 11-12).

A seemingly repetitive statement asserts that rules must be applied equally to non-Israelites and Israelites (vv. 13-16). Such a parity has already been required for Passover observance in 9:14 (cf. Exod. 12:49). One may imagine various circumstances in which such an emphatic insistence on parity would have become important. It could have been addressed primarily to non-Israelites who wanted to participate in Israelite worship on some

93

partial basis, without subjecting themselves to the full ritual and economic consequences of participation. Since the law is given to Israel, however, the rule may well have been addressed to Israelites who wanted to hold aliens living among them to a higher standard of offering, or to prevent them from participating at all in Israel's worship. Thus for all of its insistence on parity, the trajectory of this regulation is toward greater inclusiveness of those who seek to worship the God of Israel.

Discussions throughout Christian history about "fencing the communion table" are in some ways analogous to this ancient Israelite concern for participation by resident aliens in worship. What minimum standard must an "out-group" person meet in order to share in worship with those who are setting the rules? In Christian tradition, the "alien" might be the person baptized as an infant seeking to participate in a congregation that practices adult baptism, or the Protestant wondering about participation in Roman Catholic mass. In response to overtures from those on the outside, religious communities set their boundaries and standards for participation in worship. The testimony of this text to a balance between parity of requirement and inclusiveness in intention may serve as a resource for considering such boundaries and standards.

15:17-21   A gift of the firstfruits of the harvest is prescribed in Lev. 23:9-14 (cf. Deut. 26:1-2). Here this concept is extended from the gathering of the grain to the bread-making process itself. An offering is to be given from the first batch of dough made from the new grain of the harvest season. Possibly this regulation incorporated city-dwellers and other nonfarmers into the obligation and privilege of offering a portion of the harvest to God.

15:22-31   Regulations for the expiation of unintentional infractions of the law are given to supplement much more extensive regulations in Lev. 4–5. Numbers 15:22-26 concerns inadvertent error by the whole community (the "you" of v. 22 is plural in Hebrew), while vv. 27-31 concern error by individuals. The requirement of accompanying grain and drink offerings (v. 24) is added to the ritual requirements of Lev. 4–5, as is the emphasis that resident aliens are included in this legislation (Num. 15:26, 29, 30). Both additions are in accordance with the immediately preceding section of ch. 15. According to later Jewish tradition, inadvertence included both actions done without knowledge of the law and also actions based on factual misinformation (e.g., eating a forbidden part of an animal because one thought it was another part) (Levine, *Numbers 1–20*, 395). Thus purity of the sacred community can be maintained within a framework of complicated regulations. These verses conclude with a solemn reminder of the seriousness of deliberate offenses, for which perpetrators may be "cut off from among the people" (see commentary on 9:13). Such sins and their penalty must be taken with utmost seriousness even though God is understood to be One whose forgiveness ultimately outlasts wrath (see commentary on 6:25 and 14:1-10).

15:32-36 Although the outcome is clear, the crux of the incident reported here is not self-evident. Working on the sabbath was prohibited by the Decalogue (Exod. 20:10). Exodus 31:14 prescribes the death penalty for breaking the sabbath; Exod. 35:2-3 reiterates this penalty and specifies kindling a fire on the sabbath as an instance of working on the sabbath. Why did the leaders not know what to do about the man gathering sticks on the sabbath, so that they had to wait for instruction from God? Were they unsure whether the person had violated the sabbath, whether gathering sticks was permitted or not? Or were they unsure of the proper penalty for violation of the sabbath? Or were they unsure of how the death penalty should be carried out?

In the canonical form of the Pentateuch, the death penalty for violation of the sabbath by lighting a fire is already established in Exod. 35:2-3. One might suppose, therefore, that the story is intended to show that gathering sticks is work, just like making a fire. On the other hand, the immediately preceding paragraph has provided for expiation for unintentional violations of the commandments. If the community did not know whether gathering sticks violated the sabbath, then one would expect the divine response to clarify the law rather than simply pronounce the death penalty. The phrase "what should be done to him" and the focus of God's words upon the penalty suggest that the offense was clear but the correct penalty was unknown. In the canonical form of the Pentateuch, the specification of death by stoning outside the camp is thus the new information offered by God's reply. In the earlier development and remembering of individual traditions, however, this story may well have served to expand the range of sabbath-breaking work from fire-building to wood-gathering.

15:37-41   These few verses have played an important role in Jewish clothing traditions down through the centuries. Some contemporary observant Jews, for example, adapt this prescription for the four corners of the garment to Western clothing by wearing blue cords extending several inches from the two front and two back pockets of a pair of blue jeans. The legislation is understood (though the text is not explicit) to apply only to men, not to women. Like the summaries of the law tied to wrists and forehead and attached to the doorpost prescribed in Deut. 6:6-9, the tassels (or fringes) and cords remind their wearers of their commitment to serve God faithfully. Many Christian groups through the centuries and even today have prescribed items of clothing that serve this same function.

CHAPTER 16

The story recounted here continues the theme of contested leadership introduced in Num. 12–14. Although it is less familiar than the previous narratives, it stands alongside them as a text of great dramatic impact. For many modern readers, however, this impact is obscured by tensions and seeming confusion in the text. A brief background explanation may allow the power of the received story to shine through.

Two stories of revolt against the leadership of Moses and Aaron are intertwined in this chapter. One features Korah, a Levite of the Kohathite subgroup; the second features Dathan and Abiram of the Reubenite tribe. (In 16:1 a third Reubenite named On is mentioned with Dathan and Abiram, but his name does not appear again in the narrative.) The two stories have been melded together in the received form of the text by the introduction in v. 1 and by the repeated combination of the three key names in vv. 24 and 27a. The dramatic punishment described in vv. 27b-35 further unites the two stories. In the received form of the tradition, it appears that Korah's household is swallowed up by the earth, but his 250 followers are consumed by fire; the fate of Dathan and Abiram is not spelled out, but is surely to be understood from context as being swallowed up like Korah, as is remembered in Deut. 11:6 and Ps. 106:17.

The challenges to leadership presented here are multiple and do not always appear to correlate neatly with the two main groups of opponents. In general Dathan and Abiram object to the leadership of Moses, while Korah and his company object to the special role of Aaron. Moses and Aaron are brought together at least partly because Moses has the responsibility for defending Aaron's prerogatives as priestly leader. The lack of clarity centers on the "company of Korah" (Num. 16:5, 6, etc.) and their relationship to the 250 men mentioned in v. 2. In v. 2 these men are viewed as leaders of the congregation, presumably from various tribes, and their complaint in v. 3 suggests a broad populist movement. But when Moses replies to "Korah and all his company," he addresses them as "you Levites" (vv. 7c, 10). This form of address suggests a dispute between Levites and Aaronids over leadership prerogatives (see Introduction). For this reason many scholars posit two versions of the Korah story, one a more general protest, and one focusing narrowly on the Levites. The ending of the story resolves the internal tension by stating broadly that no one except descendants of the Aaronic line may offer incense (v. 40). The power of Aaron's censer and atoning intervention for the entire community is established (v. 48).

16:1-3   The story opens with a confrontation in which the rebellious groups are pictured as a single unit, "confronting" Moses, but speaking to both Moses and Aaron. The genealogy of Levi in Exod. 6:16-25 remembers Korah as a first cousin of Moses and Aaron. Dathan and Abiram are mentioned elsewhere only in reference to this story. The man called On appears only in this introduction to the chapter. The substance of the complaint is a modified and expanded version of the complaint of Miriam and Aaron in Num. 12:2 ("Has the LORD spoken only through Moses?"). Here the complainants suggest that everyone is equal before God and that God is equally present to all. Thus no special prerogatives should belong to either the prophetic or the priestly leader. The complaint is also reminiscent of Moses' words in 11:29, "Would that all the LORD's people were prophets. . . ." Here, however, Moses' response to the theme of shared responsibility is different.

16:4-11   In the first of several responses to the opening complaint, Moses addresses "Korah and all his company" (16:5-7). They are assigned a test involving censers filled with fire and incense. Moses' expression "you have gone too far" (v. 7) deliberately recalls the same phrase used by the complainants

(v. 3), as does his insistence that God will determine who is "holy" (v. 5). Moses adds a specific address to Korah (vv. 8-11) in which he attacks the Levites for trying to usurp the duties of the Aaronic priesthood. The proper role of the Levites as assistants to the Aaronids and as a buffer between the Aaronids and the people has been established earlier in Numbers, especially in 4:20 and 8:19-22. Moses emphasizes that the rebellion is against the LORD (16:11), not merely against Aaron as a human being.

16:12-15 Moses next summons Dathan and Abiram, but they refuse to appear. Their speech attacks Moses in bitter language, describing Egypt (!) as a land "flowing with milk and honey" and insisting that Moses has done the people no good but only harm. Their words "Is it too little . . ." (v. 13) lift up against Moses his own words in his speech to Korah (v. 9). The themes of death in the wilderness and lack of an inheritance of a good land are reminiscent of the challenge to Moses' leadership in 14:2-3. In the overall narrative sequence, the objection of Dathan and Abiram may be understood as a refusal to accept the judgment on the first generation pronounced in ch. 14. In this section of ch. 16 the complaint about holiness and privilege found in the beginning of the chapter is not present; the focus is on Moses' alleged failure to produce the promised results of his leadership.

Moses' angry response urges God not to accept the offerings of Dathan and Abiram. For God to refuse their offerings would mean that all communication between the rebels and God would be cut off. Moses also insists that he has not even misappropriated a single donkey (v. 15). The prophet Samuel also establishes the quality of his leadership by insisting he has not taken anyone's work animal (1 Sam. 12:3); such expressions were probably stock symbolic expressions of innocence.

16:16-19 Another round of speech to Korah develops details of the test announced in Num. 16:6-7, clarifying that Aaron's censer shall be placed alongside that of Korah and the 250 others. This paves the way for Aaron's vindication. Here the Levites are not mentioned, as Korah assembles the whole sacral community against the leaders (v. 19a NRSV). Some translators suppose that only Korah's followers are meant here (so REB; Levine, *Numbers 1-20*, 408), since v. 22 may suggest that the congregation as a whole was innocent. In favor of the NRSV translation is the assumption in v. 21 that the entire congregation is near Moses and Aaron. As elsewhere, the appearance of the glory of the LORD signifies a major turning point (cf. 12:5; 14:10).

16:20-35   God's initial proposal to destroy everyone except the two leaders (16:21) is averted by the intercession of the leaders who urge that the innocent not be punished along with the guilty. This rationale is distinctive and unusual within the OT, although it stands within a larger context of intercessory prayer. A pattern of intercession that averts a more severe divine judgment, especially the total annihilation of the people, has been seen already in ch. 14. It appears also in the prophetic literature, notably in Amos' prayers that his visions of destruction will not come to pass (Amos 7, although in Amos the declaration of general judgment is not finally withdrawn). In Num. 14 and Amos, however, the intercession is on behalf of a guilty community, with the goal of reducing or averting the penalty, whereas in 16:22 the argument is based on the innocence of some of the people. This latter theme is reminiscent of Abraham's effort to intervene on behalf of Sodom (Gen. 18:22-33), but again there are important differences. The Abraham story seeks to save all the guilty on the basis of the innocence of a few. Here, however, the result of the prayer is to limit the punishment to those who overtly spoke against Moses. On the surface such a limitation resembles the assertion of Ezek. 18 that people shall die for their own sin, but in Ezekiel the focus is that guilt will not be transmitted from one generation to the next; distinction among individuals within a group of contemporaries is not in the foreground.

God's revised command (Num. 16:24) requires the main congregation to put some physical distance between themselves and the rebels. Moses declares that his authority as God's representative is to be vindicated by the sudden and unusual death of his detractors (v. 29). So it happens, just as Moses had said: "the earth opened its mouth and swallowed them up" (v. 32). The frightened Israelites flee, and fire consumes the 250.

As noted above, internal tensions in this description of the judgment reveal a conflation of traditions. Dathan and Abiram are called to stand at their tents, and they are the opponents of Moses according to vv. 12-15. But only Korah and his family are explicitly mentioned as being swallowed up; thus Korah here is separated from his company of 250 who are consumed by fire.

The concept of the earth swallowing up the enemies of God is found also in the ancient Song of the Sea, Exod. 15:12. It is probably best to understand this theme poetically as a display of God's power beyond human explaining, rather than to create some "naturalistic" explanation such as an earthquake crack that recloses over its victims. Sheol (Num. 16:30) is the most common Hebrew term for the dwelling place of the dead. It is thought of as very low, below the earth, and is a place of watery silence and darkness from which there is no escape. Although Sheol is often mentioned in connection with the wicked, the patriarch Jacob speaks of going to Sheol (Gen. 37:35). Several Psalms speak of Sheol in connection with the presumably upright psalmist who desires to be rescued from death in order to praise God (e.g., Ps. 6:5; 18:5). Thus, by contrast to the later Christian idea of hell, Sheol is not a special place of punishment reserved for the wicked.

16:36-40   This section of the story serves primarily to explain the significance of a certain bronze covering for the altar. Made from the censers of the 250 men consumed by the fire, this covering is to serve as a reminder that God has confirmed the special prerogative of Aaron's line. Just as the opening up of the earth confirmed Moses' authority, so the fire consuming the men whose censers were not chosen confirmed Aaron's authority. Since the bronze covering is a reminder for "the Israelites," not just for the Levites, this conclusion moves back to the community-wide challenge represented in Num. 16:3 and 19.

The responsibility for scattering the fire and remaking the censers of the dead complainants into this bronze covering is assigned to the priest Eleazar. Eleazar is the son of Aaron, and is eventually Aaron's successor (see ch. 20). No reason for this assignment is expressed. It seems likely, however, that concern for contamination through contact with an object associated with dead persons, and especially with dead rebels, may lie in the background. Every effort would be made to avoid contamination of Aaron as the high priest (cf. Lev. 21:10-11 and commentary on Num. 19:1-10 and 12:10-16).

16:41-50 Despite the sign of the bronze plating reminding that the complainants had been in the wrong, the entire congregation promptly rebels. The whole congregation may not have been present at the previous rebellion and judgment, or may have been only passive witnesses to it (see discussion of 16:19-22). Now they are clearly in active opposition, blaming Moses and Aaron for the death of the others. As in v. 19, the glory of the LORD appears, and as in v. 21 God expresses an intention to destroy the whole congregation. This time Moses does not pray but sends Aaron out to halt the destroying plague that is already underway. The presence of Aaron who carries his incense censer and makes atonement halts the spread of death; the power of Aaron and the drama of the moment are portrayed as a line drawn at Aaron's feet between the living and the dead (v. 48). The halting of the "plague" by Aaron's "making atonement" draws the reader back to 8:19, where it is the function of the Levites as assistants to Aaron to "make atonement," thus averting "plague." Since a rebellion among Levites (16:7) seeking to usurp Aaronic authority had been the root cause of the plague of v. 46, Aaron now must step into the breach and deliver the people. Atonement becomes the responsibility of the Aaronic line, and Aaron's special authority is further confirmed.

As the Introduction suggests, the insistence upon special authority for the Aaronic line may well be a development that occurred late in Israel's history as a people, as late as the Second Temple period. Stories such as this one may therefore not be literal representations of events of the wilderness era, but efforts of the later community to ascribe the settlement of all leadership disputes to ancient times. The possibility that the stories are later creations (or at least heavily reworked traditions) and are not factual in every detail does not, however, compromise their value; the goal is to give expression through story to the theological idea that God designates leadership for the community and expects the community to honor rather than to overthrow its divinely appointed leadership. The story, however, is told with the benefit of hindsight. In the everyday struggles of communities of faith, it is often not so easy to be sure which leaders are genuinely of God. This story of the rejection of those claiming leadership should not be separated from the contrasting story of Eldad and Medad (11:26-30), whose unexpected gift of leadership was confirmed despite the objection of another leader.

CHAPTER 17

At God's command twelve staffs are placed in the sacred tent, one for each tribe with a leader's name written on it. Aaron's name is written on a staff representing Levi, and some scholars find in 17:6 an indication that Aaron's is a thirteenth staff. The next day, the staffs are brought out for inspection. Aaron's staff has sprouted buds, produced blossoms, and borne ripe almonds. This staff is replaced in the sanctuary as a warning against rebellion. Then the people wonder how they can approach for worship.

God's command concerning the staffs seems to have two purposes. On the one hand, all the Israelites see that Aaron's rod has blossomed. This serves to confirm yet again his individual authority in the face of the challenges described in the previous chapter. On the other hand, a story of twelve staffs, with Aaron's name representing the tribe of Levi, suggests that it is the Levitical tribe as a whole with its special role of religious leadership that is being set apart here. This too may look back to the previous dispute in which the complainants claimed that everyone was equally holy (16:3). Once this claim is rejected, the people lament that they have no access to the sanctuary, on pain of death (17:12-13). This lament seems to have been taken care of by all the instructions for the Levites in ch. 8. In this context, though, it apparently serves to introduce the material of ch. 18 on the duties of priests and Levites.

· CHAPTER 18

18:1-7   Here God addresses Aaron alone (vv. 1, 8, 20). Elsewhere in Exodus through Deuteronomy (with the exception of
the Decalogue, addressed to the whole people; Exod. 20) God
speaks only to Moses, or to Moses and Aaron together. Appropriately, the topic of this unique speech to Aaron is responsibilities
of the priesthood. The duties of priests and of Levites are stated.
This material reiterates what has been announced earlier, especially in Num. 8, about the relationship between the two groups.
The priests alone may have contact with the altar, the utensils,
and the area behind the curtain. The Levites are to assist them
at the sanctuary, avoiding contact with the most holy objects.
Outsiders (other Israelites and non-Israelites) are barred from
approaching on penalty of death, but this restriction is not viewed
negatively. Rather, the arrangement presented here meets the
concerns of the community expressed in 17:12-13. The idea that
death will result from improper incursion into sacred space is an
ancient taboo, known in many cultures. The story of Uzzah's
death upon touching the ark of the covenant (2 Sam. 6:6-7) is
an Israelite narrative that illustrates this taboo.

18:8-20   The financial support of the priesthood is summarized
in a review of the portions of the various sacrifices and offerings that
are available to the priests and their families for food. In each case
the portion to be eaten is to be distinguished from the parts offered
to the deity. Portions of certain "most holy things" may be eaten
only by the priests themselves ("every male"; Num. 18:8-10);
portions of other offerings may be eaten by the entire families of
the priests (explicitly including daughters) who are ritually clean (vv.

11-19). Within the section detailing food available to the entire family, the regulations concerning redemption of the firstborn are reviewed (see Exod. 13:2; 22:29b-30; 34:19-20; Num. 3:11-13); here earlier regulations are modified by provision for cash redemption for the firstborn of an unclean animal.

The expression "covenant of salt" in the concluding summary (18:19) appears elsewhere only in Lev. 2:13 and 2 Chr. 13:5. The former applies the term to the relationship between God and people; the latter, to God and the house of David. Here the terminology is more vague, as the phrase does not explicitly apply to the relationship between the priests and God. Salt is used both positively and negatively in the texts of various treaties known from the ancient Near East; the exact meaning in these biblical passages is not certain. In this case, the perpetual character of the regulation is probably the central feature. The paragraph concludes with a reminder that the priests, as part of the Levitical tribe, have no land allotment (Num. 18:20).

18:21-32   The Levites' duties and food portions are described in a format similar to that for the priesthood in the opening sections of the chapter. Verses 21-24 summarize their situation: the tithes are their payment (v. 21); they shall serve in the sanctuary in place of the ordinary Israelites (vv. 22-23a); they shall have no land allotment (vv. 23b-24).

Detail concerning the tithe as the designated source of income for the Levites is spelled out in vv. 25ff. This is new information, not a summary or modification of some previous legislation. It is directed to the Levites. In this context it is notable that God's words are once again addressed to the recipients through Moses. This represents a return to the normal channel of communication, to which vv. 1-24 are the exception. The rationale for the "tithe of the tithe" that the Levites must set apart as their offering to the LORD (v. 29) suggests a rationale for the regulation concerning tithing of bread dough in 15:17-21 (see commentary). All Israelites are expected to tithe the "firstfruits" of their daily bread, whatever its source. Since the Levites receive grain and wine from many different harvests, they must select the best (18:29), rather than the first received, as the tenth that they offer to God.

CHAPTER 19

This chapter provides details of the procedures for purification in case of contact with a dead body. The opening paragraph (19:1-10) gives instruction for preparation of ashes to be used in the purification rites. These instructions are followed by general (vv. 11-13) and more specific (vv. 14-22) instructions concerning purification.

19:1-10 The entire ceremony for preparation of the ashes, as well as the storage of the ashes and use of them for purification, takes place outside the camp. An unblemished red cow is to be slaughtered in the presence of the priest Eleazar, son of Aaron. Although this is described as a one-time event, it is understood that the ashes from this first animal will not last forever; so this instruction is intended as a model for such preparations in the future.

Some English translations call this animal a "heifer," i.e., a female that has not given birth to a calf. That the animal is young might be inferred from the requirement that it has never worn a yoke (v. 2). The Hebrew word itself does not require that the animal is a heifer (see 1 Sam. 6:7). Leviticus 22:21-25 gives the basic requirements for the category "unblemished." According to some later Jewish traditions, an "unblemished" red cow must also have no more than two hairs that are not red, an obvious rarity in the animal world. It is likely that the red color of the animal is related to the theme of blood.

After the animal is killed, the priest dashes a little of its blood seven times in the direction of the sacred tent. In this Priestly text the tent is probably thought of as in the center of the camp.

All of the heifer is to be burned, even its blood and its dung; no other ritual recorded in the Pentateuch requires such complete burning of the animal. Cedarwood, hyssop, and crimson material are to be added to the fire, thus becoming part of the resultant ash. The same three ingredients are mentioned in connection with a different purification ceremony in Lev. 14:1-7; the precise significance of these ingredients is not certain.

Numbers 19:7-10 indicates that at least three people are required for the ritual preparation of the ashes: the priest who is responsible for the ritual details described in vv. 4-6, another individual responsible for the actual burning, and a third person to gather up the ashes and deposit them in the appointed "clean place" outside the camp. (Whether the person who slaughters the animal, v. 3, is a fourth person or is the same as the one who burns it cannot be determined from the text; but the absence of instruction concerning purification of the slaughterer may suggest that he is also the one who does the burning.) The priest certainly is male, and both grammar and culture suggest that the other participants in the preparation of the ashes are also male. Each of these three persons is rendered ritually impure by participating in the ceremony; each must undergo a rite of purification by water after completing the designated assignment. This period of ritual impurity is the likely explanation for assigning the priestly role to Eleazar, rather than to Aaron; any contamination of the high priest was to be avoided (cf. Lev. 21:10-11 and commentary on Num. 16:36-40 and 12:10-16). The priest and the one responsible for burning the animal must wash both their clothing and their bodies; the one gathering the ashes washes only his clothing. Although all three alike become clean in the evening, the difference in washing requirements may indicate a difference in degree of defilement between those involved in the burning and the one gathering the ashes.

Numbers 19:10b appears at first glance to be a stereotypical summation, except that in this case no content of the law is reviewed. The emphasis is upon inclusion of the non-Israelite resident alien in these regulations. But the regulations that could reasonably pertain to the resident alien are found in the following sections, not in the description of preparation of the ashes. Thus

v. 10b provides a transition to the next section and is appropriately treated in some translations (e.g., NRSV) as introductory to the following instructions for use of the ashes. The intent here is to place all those who identify themselves with Israel and live in its midst geographically under the requirements of the following purification legislation.

19:11-13   The general rule for contact with a dead body of a human being is stated. Verse 11 specifies that uncleanness results from touching any human corpse. Although later Jewish tradition restricted the need for purification to persons having contact with the dead body of a Jewish person (Levine, *Numbers 1–20*, 465), 31:19 presumes uncleanness even for warriors who have touched an enemy corpse. Seven days of impurity result from contact with any human corpse, and rites of purification must be undertaken on the third and seventh days. The penalty for ignoring the requirements is severe. Those who defile the tabernacle by failing to observe these rites will be "cut off from Israel." It is not known exactly how this penalty, mentioned frequently in Priestly legislation, was practiced. The basic meaning of being "cut off" was probably banishment from the community, although it may have been softened to loss of status or some kind of shunning. It is possible that the focus on the defilement of the tabernacle (19:13; cf. "the sanctuary of the LORD," v. 20) offers a clue to the placement of this chapter within the book. Chapter 18 deals with various duties of the priests and Levites for preserving the sanctity and holiness of the tent of meeting. The general populace is to keep its distance (18:22) while the Levites act on their behalf. But the sacred space could still be violated, according to ch. 19, by the presence, even at a distance, of any Israelite who had not undergone purification for contact with a dead body. Hence the theme of the sanctity of the tent of meeting or tabernacle is continued here.

19:14-22   The regulations are spelled out in detail. Uncleanness is incurred by contact whether the body is in a tent or in an open field, whether the death is of natural causes or through violence; even contact with a grave or a bone results in uncleanness. It is also apparent that the uncleanness is not restricted to those having actual physical contact with the corpse. Anyone who is in or comes into a tent where there is a corpse becomes unclean. Furthermore, inanimate objects, namely open containers (v. 15) and even a tent and its furnishings (v. 18), become unclean from the presence of a dead human body.

The cleansing ritual is not complicated. A clean person mixes some of the ritually prepared ashes with running water in a container. ("Running water" means stream or spring water as opposed to cistern water.) The person then uses a hyssop sprig to sprinkle the water on any unclean persons and objects. The unclean persons are to be sprinkled in this way on the third and seventh days; then they wash their clothes and bodies and become clean on the evening of the seventh day. The description of the procedure concludes with an elaboration of the penalty for disregarding the requirement of purification (v. 20).

After a concluding summation (v. 21a) additional details concerning states of uncleanness are provided. In parallel with the clean person who gathered the original ashes, the clean person who prepares the water and sprinkles it becomes unclean for that day but is required only to wash his clothing, not his body. Anyone else (who was clean) who touches the water is unclean for that day but is apparently not required to perform any ritual (v. 21b). Objects touched by an unclean person become unclean and can temporarily contaminate persons who touch them; but apparently such persons also are not required to perform any ritual (v. 22). One can readily imagine that these verses were added as clarifying postscripts in response to questions about application of the preceding regulation.

CHAPTER 20

The theme of ch. 20 is the death of the three leaders of the original generation departing from Egypt. The deaths of Miriam and Aaron are recorded here. Of course, in the received form of the tradition, Moses' death does not take place until the end of the book of Deuteronomy.

20:1   The chapter opens with an announcement of the people's arrival at the wilderness of Zin. This is the first schematized geographic notice of moving of the Israelite camp since the end of ch. 12, where the people moved to the wilderness of Paran. There is some confusion in the details of these geographic notices. Here Kadesh is presented as if it were a part of the wilderness of Zin. In 13:26 it is thought of as part of the wilderness of Paran, which is slightly further south. Modern atlases place Kadesh differently on their maps, depending upon which of these two traditions they follow. The story of the failed invasion (14:39-45) portrays the people being driven back as far as Hormah, which is north of the wilderness of Zin; but it is easy to suppose that the Israelites retreated further than they were pursued. These tensions in geographic detail probably reflect different ancient traditions about the progress of the people through the wilderness. In any case, the camp is now set in the northeastern area of the Sinai Peninsula.

The date similarly is unclear, since the "first month" is not attached to any year. George Buchanan Gray (*Numbers,* 259-260) proposes that the date is the fortieth year and that the number has been omitted because of the tension in the double reference to Kadesh in 13:26 and 20:1. The resumption of the march toward

111

the land begins in 20:14, which must be understood as the end of the traditional forty years in the wilderness. The question is only whether the intervening years lie between ch. 14 and the beginning of ch. 20, or between 20:1 and 20:14; the chronological ambiguity here corresponds redactionally to the geographic ambiguity about Kadesh.

The death of Miriam and her burial are recorded in a single sentence. The death of the older sister — who according to tradition helped save the baby Moses (though her name is not recorded in Exod. 2), who led Israel in song after the deliverance at the Red Sea (Exod. 15:20-21), who was of such stature in the community that she was remembered to have offered a serious challenge to Moses' authority (Num. 12) — is reported without comment. Miriam disappears from the narrative without so much as a word about the mourning of her departure from life. No details of any sort are offered about her passing.

Nonetheless, within the androcentric circles that preserved the wilderness traditions, her death is in fact recorded rather than ignored; and its narrative location gives to Miriam a certain standing within the memories of Israel. The immediately following narrative explains why neither Moses nor Aaron is able to lead the people into the Promised Land. The report of Miriam's death as the "heading" for this narrative suggests that the three leaders are to be remembered together in death even as they functioned together in life. Miriam's leadership is tacitly recognized by the placement of her death notice alongside those of her brothers.

20:2-13 This passage concerns water from the rock and God's judgment upon Moses and Aaron for their sin in handling the people's request for water. The story is in some way related to the earlier story of water from the rock recorded in Exod. 17, although there Aaron does not play a role. Various grammatical and narrative tensions in Num. 20:2-13 seem to be occasioned by the inclusion of Aaron alongside of Moses in this story. The Hebrew shows an inconsistent pattern of singular and plural verbs, both in the divine command and in the leaders' response. The ownership of the staff is not clear: v. 9 appears to refer to Aaron's budding staff of ch. 17, but "his" staff in 20:11a refers to Moses.

Commentators have sometimes explained these and other difficulties by regarding Aaron as a late addition to the narrative. The
apparent difficulties are equally well explained, however, by understanding this passage as an effort to balance the relationship
between the two leaders in this their final joint appearance in the
narrative (Katharine Doob Sakenfeld, "Theological and Redactional Problems in Numbers 20:2-13").

The story is the last of a long sequence in which the two leaders
have appeared together, beginning with God's instruction to
Moses about the role of Aaron in Exod. 4:14-17. From beginning
to end not only the relationship between two individuals needs
to be defined, but also the relationship between the priestly and
prophetic roles. The role of those in the line of Aaron who preserve
the ritual purity of the community has to be separated from the
role of those in the line of Moses who bring God's word to that
same community. Here Aaron appears in an "equal yet subordinate" role, as indeed he is seen in the larger picture in the Priestly
tradition. Moses' use of Aaron's rod points the reader in the
direction of Aaron's subordination, as does Moses' exclusive receiving of divine address even when Aaron is present with him.

On the other hand, the two are equal in their participation in
the sin that leads to their judgment. Although the text does not
specify that Aaron "did" any particular act, except helping to
gather the people, Num. 20:12 makes clear that the two are held
fully and equally accountable for whatever took place. This emphasis on equality or balance is carried forward in the subsequent
accounts of the deaths of Aaron and Moses, where plural verbs
are used in the statements of reason for their deaths (v. 24;
27:13-14; Deut. 32:50-51). The stories of the installation of
Eleazar as successor to Aaron (20:26-28) and of Joshua as successor to Moses (27:18-23) further express the interrelatedness of
the priestly and prophetic lines of leadership.

What is the sin of Moses and Aaron that results in their
disqualification as leaders? Looking at the narrative as a whole,
one can see that their first two actions (taking the staff and
assembling the congregation) correspond to the first two items
in God's commands. Then one leader speaks to the people and
Moses strikes the rock. Neither of these acts is specifically in

accord with the divine command, yet neither openly contradicts it; 20:12 does not specify the wrongdoing it condemns. Many proposals have therefore been put forward concerning the content of the leaders' sin. While the striking of the rock might be regarded as wrong since it was not explicitly commanded, the content of the question addressed to the people (v. 10) is more evidently inappropriate.

The Hebrew form of the question can have three possible nuances. First, it may be simply open-ended: "Shall we (or shall we not) bring forth water?" In this tone the question would expect the people to beg the leaders for water, despite God's command to provide them with water. Alternatively, the question may expect a negative answer, as in "Can we bring forth water?" In such form the wording invites the people to disbelieve in the power of God given to Moses and Aaron, or else suggests Moses' and Aaron's own disbelief. Third, the question can be taken as a rhetorical form of indignant refusal: "Shall we indeed?! Why should we . . . ?" The context is too limited to determine which of these three nuances is intended. But on any of these three interpretations, the very speaking of the question takes away from the holiness of God and of the occasion itself. The unfaithful content of the question is thus the likeliest reason for the judgment of God upon Moses and Aaron.

As has been noted, the question answered here is not why Moses and Aaron are not allowed to enter the land, but why they are not allowed to *lead* the people into the land (v. 12). Whether prophet or priest, those who tempt the people not to trust in God, those whose leadership diverts the people's attention from the presence of the Holy One in their midst, are not suitable leaders of God's people.

20:14-21   The end of the wilderness era is at hand, and Moses prepares to lead the people toward Transjordan. The obvious route is through the territory of Edom lying at the southern end of the Dead Sea, and Moses sends a request for passage to the Edomite king. The appeal is based on several factors, and careful conditions are set forth. Moses suggests they are "brothers" (v. 14), perhaps referring to the tradition that Jacob's brother Esau was the ancestor of the Edomites (Gen. 36:9). Israel's history as an oppressed people delivered is mentioned as if to curry sympathy, and the convenience of the route ("here we are at your border") is lifted up. Moses pledges that there will be no damage to Edom's economy. Israel will stick to the King's Highway (the main trade route through Transjordan in ancient times, connecting the Gulf of Aqabah and Damascus). No well-water or food will be consumed. Nonetheless, Edom rejects Israel's request, threatening to use force if necessary to prevent Israel's passage. Moses then offers to pay for any water needed (probably a more realistic suggestion than the claim that none will be used). Edom responds by carrying out its threat, sending armed forces to guard its borders. This outcome may be reflected in Amos' judgment upon Edom who "pursued his brother with the sword" (Amos 1:11).

The picture of Edom in these verses does not fit well with what is known archaeologically of this geographic location and its inhabitants in the late second millennium (Burton MacDonald, "Archaeology of Edom"). Thus, whatever the nature of the encounter between Israel and Edom in this early period, the story has been retold in a way that reflects first-millennium conditions in that region.

20:22-29   Aaron dies at Mt. Hor, the first stop on the journey detouring around Edom. God reiterates the reason that Aaron will die outside the land (cf. Num. 20:2-13) and provides instruction for the installation of Eleazar as Aaron's successor. The people see the three men go up the mountain. Out of sight of the people waiting at the foot of the mountain, Moses vests Eleazar with Aaron's robes of office and Aaron dies. The people see that Moses and Eleazar return without Aaron, and a period of mourning results.

The parallels to the death of Moses as recorded (probably by a Priestly writer) in Deut. 34 should be noted. Each leader dies atop a mountain, out of view of the people, whither he has gone at the command of God. The burial place of Aaron is not mentioned; that of Moses is unknown. Each is mourned for thirty days. The balance between the priestly and prophetic fountain-heads is preserved in the accounts of their deaths.

CHAPTER 21

Numbers 21 recounts incidents in the journey from Mt. Hor to the plains of Moab opposite Jericho (22:1). Many of the places mentioned cannot be identified with certainty. Because of this, scholarly maps showing possible routes for Israel's journey to Transjordan do not agree in detail and must be regarded as provisional. Four events are sketched in ch. 21: battle with the king of Arad (vv. 1-3); poisonous serpents (vv. 4-9); battle with King Sihon of the Amorites (vv. 21-31); and battle with King Og of Bashan (vv. 33-35). Three fragments of ancient songs are also incorporated into the chapter (vv. 14-15, 17-18, 27-30).

21:1-3   The Israelites are attacked by a Canaanite king from Arad. The Israelites vow to utterly destroy everything that comes into their possession from the enemy. After this vow, God gives them victory, and the place (whether a town or region) is renamed Hormah, a play on the Hebrew word for "destruction."

Archaeologists have shown that the site known as Tell Arad was not occupied during the Late Bronze period, so there are difficulties in placing this king of Arad in the wilderness era. However that is explained, the main point in the received form of the story is probably the contrast between this experience and the one recorded in 14:39-45. In the earlier story, the Israelites disobediently attempted to take the land (against God's decree of forty years in the wilderness). This led to military defeat at a place named Hormah. Here the same place name Hormah becomes associated with military victory as the people set out toward the land at the end of the forty years.

21:4-9 This story of the fiery or poisonous serpents is a compact account of a further rebellion or complaint of the people, the theme that occupies much of chs. 11–18. The end of the wandering era and the beginning of the march toward the Promised Land (21:1-3) does not mean an end to complaining.

Various theories have been proposed concerning the relationship between these verses and the notice of the destruction of Moses' bronze serpent in the Jerusalem temple hundreds of years later during the reign of King Hezekiah (2 Kgs. 18:4). During the time of Hezekiah, the people had been making offerings to the bronze serpent. Hezekiah seems to have been trying to destroy an object that was functioning like an idol or like an image forbidden by the Decalogue. The Numbers text may simply describe the origin of that cult object neutrally, without intending any reference to the bronze serpent's use or misuse in the temple. On the other hand, Numbers may be intended to establish the original positive significance of the cult object, thus absolving Moses of guilt in its manufacture. The intent of the text is difficult to determine because this symbol is not referred to elsewhere in the OT and because this passage is very difficult to date.

Scholarly literature also offers many theories about the cultural background of the healing power associated with the snake symbol. Hypotheses have been offered based on comparisons to snake symbolism in Egypt, Canaan, Mesopotamia, and later Greece. Certainly the motif was widespread in the ancient world.

The narrative of Num. 21:4-9 begins with complaint. The seemingly illogical complaint ("there is no food . . . we detest this miserable food") represents a summary of the previous complaints of Exod. 16 and 17 and Num. 11 and 20. The story moves to judgment, with the biting snakes and death. Repentance from the people follows, and Moses intercedes. God gives instruction, and then Moses acts. Those who gaze upon the bronze serpent on its pole survive. The sequence seems a fuller version of the complaining at Taberah (11:1-3) except that here the ending is different. Whereas in 11:3 the fire "abated" after Moses' intercession, here the text gives no indication that the snakes themselves were taken away. The Hebrew of 21:9b is ambiguous. It could refer just to the healing of those already bitten before the intercession; but it can also include the possibility of healing for those bitten subsequently, as indicated by the NRSV translation.

The requirement that those bitten look at the bronze serpent in order to be healed brings another nuance to the understanding of divine forgiveness and restoration (see commentary on 14:11-38 and 16:20-35, 41-50). Here the healing is made available, but it does not happen directly or to the whole community because of group repentance and Moses' intercession. Rather, healing takes place in individuals, in response to their act of looking at the bronze figure. God provides the means of healing, yet some level of personal human believing and initiative is required for its efficacy. The motivation of individual Israelites who look at the bronze serpent and are healed remains unspecified. Even though they have admitted their sin in complaining, it is possible that desperation or even magical belief could be at work, rather than mature trust in the power of God. But whatever the motivation, healing comes with looking at the bronze serpent, as provided for by God.

This passage might well be unknown to many Christians except for the reference to it in John 3:14-15, which compares the lifting up of the Son of Man to Moses' lifting up of the serpent in the wilderness. The comparison is followed immediately by John 3:16, probably the best-known Bible verse in world Christianity. The intent of John's comparison between Jesus and the bronze serpent is not self-evident, but may be taken to refer both to the Cruci-fixion and the Resurrection (Raymond E. Brown, *The Gospel According to John I–XII. Anchor Bible* [Garden City: Doubleday, 1966], 145-46). As both John 3:15 and 3:16 state explicitly, God's purpose is to provide eternal life for those who believe. A human act of response is required for receiving this eternal life, even as the human act of looking at the bronze serpent was essential to healing in the wilderness.

21:10-20   This section contains a brief description of the stages of the journey toward Transjordan (see Num. 33). The description provides the context for incorporating two ancient poetic songs.

The first poem, 21:14-15, is cited from "the Book of the Wars of the LORD." This book is mentioned only here in the OT. Like a number of other ancient sources cited in the OT, it no longer exists. The meaning of the song is very obscure and the locations of the place names Waheb, Suphah, and Ar are not known; indeed, the first two words are obscure and textually corrupt and may not be place names at all. The song appears here because of its references to Arnon and the border of Moab, mentioned in the itinerary in v. 13.

The second song, vv. 17-18, is a song probably used to celebrate the completion of digging a well. Again, its use here is related to the appearance of the Hebrew place name Beer ("Well") in v. 16 of the itinerary.

21:21-32 These verses and the following section (vv. 33-35) present the story of the capture of the territory of King Sihon the Amorite and of his neighbor to the north, King Og of Bashan. There are formidable literary and historical-geographical problems in these stories as recounted here and in Deut. 2–3. Wide areas of overlap between the Numbers and Deuteronomy narratives are punctuated by sharp disagreements (e.g., did the Israelites immediately settle in Sihon's territory?). The borders of the territories in question are not consistently described. The ruins known today as Tell Hesban were not occupied in the Late Bronze era, so the location of Sihon's capital city is not known. These and many other problems caution against reading these texts as simple eyewitness accounts. On the other hand, evidence from archaeology and the social sciences confirms that major shifts in demographics did take place in Transjordan at the transition from the Late Bronze to the Early Iron eras (ca. 1200 B.C.E.). Despite the difficulties of these narratives, they are not to be viewed as pure invention by later writers. (For an excellent brief summation of these difficulties and possible explanations, see Robert G. Boling, *The Early Biblical Community in Transjordan*.)

The appeal by Israel to King Sihon begins much like the earlier appeal to Edom in Num. 20:14-17 (except for the absence of the term "brother" in 20:14). The outcome differs greatly, however, for battle is engaged and Sihon is defeated. Israel takes control of Sihon's territory, including some land held formerly by Moab (21:26).

This last notice about Moabite territory gives rise to the inclusion of the song in vv. 27-30. The song depicts an attack coming forth from Heshbon that engulfs Moabite territory. The defeated Moabites, described as "people of Chemosh [their god]," are pictured as men in hiding and women war captives. Severe textual difficulties make the precise meaning of v. 30 uncertain, although a bad fate for the victims of defeat seems apparent.

The origin of the song is obscure. Some argue that it is not Israelite, but was first sung by the followers of Sihon to taunt the Moabites concerning Sihon's capture of their land and people (vv. 28, 29). Others treat the song as Israelite in origin; they offer various theories to explain why Israel would compose a song about Sihon's capture of Moab. Whatever the origin of the song, Israel preserved it not just to record an ancient memory of Sihon's defeating Moab but especially as part of Israel's own tradition of negative feeling toward Moab. (Some examples of this can be found in ch. 25; Judg. 3:12-30; various battles in 1-2 Kings; and prophetic oracles against Moab.)

21:33-35   The summarized itinerary concludes with a report of the victory over King Og of Bashan and the capture of his territory. According to Deut. 3:8-11 Og's territory extended as far north as Mt. Hermon in southwestern Syria. The tradition that Og was of gigantic proportions is also recorded in Deuteronomy's review of this event.

END OF THE
FIRST GENERATION
OPPOSITE JERICHO
(22:1–25:18)

CHAPTERS 22; 23 AND 24
(PROSE SECTIONS)

The final move of the itinerary brings the Israelites to the plains of Moab (Num. 22:1), where they will remain until after the death of Moses (Deut. 34). Numbers 22–24 records a story in which the Israelites play no role at all. Indeed, although their very existence is at stake, the Israelites apparently have no idea that events affecting their destiny are underway. The narrator does not even explain how Israel came to know the story of Balaam, the diviner summoned by King Balak of Moab to curse Israel.

Chapter 22 presents a long prose prologue recounting Balak's summons to Balaam and Balaam's eventual arrival in Moabite territory. Chapters 23–24 place Balaam's four poetic utterances in a narrative context. The context reveals Balak's displeasure with the oracular content and his frustrated efforts to achieve a different result. Throughout the entire section runs the theme of the power of Israel's God and the intention of that God to protect and bless the Israelites.

Certain problems in the story should be noted even though they need not be solved in order to appreciate the narrative. The existence of a king of Moab with substantial territory seems an oddity. Numbers 21:26-30 has reported the earlier demise of Moab at the hands of Sihon the Amorite. Perhaps the extent of Sihon's victory was exaggerated, and/or Moab experienced a resurgence in the context of the disruption created by Israel.

An additional mystery concerns Balaam's role, which is not presented consistently in other biblical references. In Num. 31:16 (cf. Rev. 2:14) he is said to have led Israel into apostasy, an allegation that bears no apparent relation to the tradition here. The Num. 31 accusation comes in the context of reprisals against

Midian, however, and one notes that there are puzzling references to the Midianites in 22:4 and 7, which have no substantive role in the present form of the story. Other OT references to Balaam focus primarily on the futility of King Balak's attempt to thwart God's care for Israel (Deut. 23:4-6; Josh. 13:22; 24:9-10; Judg. 11:25; Neh. 13:2; Mic. 6:5), while the NT references take quite a different tack and criticize Balaam for trying to make a financial profit from wrongdoing (2 Pet. 2:15-16; Jude 11).

An eighth-century B.C.E. inscription from Tell Deir 'Alla (located on the east side of the Jordan Valley near the mouth of the River Jabbok) speaks of a figure named Balaam who is a seer and gives an oracle. The inscription is fragmentary and the extant text bears no direct relation to the Numbers material. Nonetheless, the existence of such an inscription (even though presumably non-Israelite) testifies to a strong tradition of the figure of Balaam in the biblical period.

22:1-14   The narrative of Num. 22 is one of the funniest in the OT, and also one of the most theologically profound. Balak, king of Moab, is terrified that Israel will overcome him "as an ox licks up the grass of the field" (v. 4), just as Israel has overcome the Amorites. He sends messengers a great distance, all the way to the Euphrates, although the exact location is debated. The messengers are to invite a certain Balaam to overcome this threat by cursing the Israelites. Balak's praise of Balaam, spoken through his messengers, indicates why he has reached out so far: "I know that whomever you bless is blessed, and whomever you curse is cursed" (v. 6). Balaam is pictured here as a diviner, i.e., one who seeks omens and pronounces blessings or curses on other people, normally for pay. His effectiveness has given him an international reputation.

The story rests on the premise that there is power in the spoken word. In the ancient world it mattered what Balaam said. People believed that what he spoke was going to happen; his words had power. The emphasis on the effectiveness of Balaam's words is part of the larger OT testimony that God uses words, intentionally spoken to effect change, as one way of bringing change in the world. God puts words in Jeremiah's mouth to set Jeremiah "over nations and over kingdoms, to pluck up and to pull down, to destroy and to overthrow, to build and to plant" (Jer. 1:10). The priest Amaziah says of Amos that "the land is not able to bear all his words" (Amos 7:10). The Israelite king says of the prophet Micaiah, "I hate him, for he never prophesies anything favorable about me, but only disaster" (1 Kgs. 22:8). This sense of the power of words spoken, particularly by designated specialists, remains lively even today in many non-Western cultures. Even Western cultures recognize such power in words, although this is seen mainly in the secular realms of advertising and of "spin doctors," public relations specialists who manipulate news stories to the advantage of their own employer or political party.

Balaam hears the offer of Balak's emissaries but says his decision must rest on what the LORD tells him to do. God tells Balaam not to go: "You shall not curse the people, for they are blessed" (Num. 22:12). Balaam reports that "the LORD has refused" him permission, and the emissaries return home to Balak with the news that "Balaam refuses."

Already in these opening scenes a key theological problem of the story has been introduced. Balaam works for pay. Yet he also consults and obeys God, who is identified in his own words as the LORD (Yahweh), i.e., Israel's God. What is the relationship between paid speaking and speaking in accord with God's plan? Why is a diviner by the Euphrates using the name of Yahweh? The tension is so obvious that many scholars recognize two major strands of tradition in this story. In one of these, Balaam is presented as a diviner who seeks omens and works for hire. The other strand of tradition is one in which Balaam is a more typical Yahweh prophet who speaks only what God commands him. While the sorting of the story into these strands is certainly plausible, the tension created by their combination has its own theological perspective to offer, as is suggested below.

22:15-21   The desperate King Balak renews his invitation to Balaam, sending a larger, more prestigious delegation to present the offer of a larger honorarium. Balaam explains that no matter what the reward, he "could not go beyond the command of the LORD [his] God, to do less or more [i.e., anything at all]" (v. 18).

But he consults God again, and this time God gives Balaam permission to make the trip, provided he does only God's bidding. Balaam saddles his donkey and the journey begins.

22:22-35   Here we encounter another anomaly in the story. God has just given Balaam permission to go to Moab (v. 20), but now God becomes angry because he is going (v. 22). The angel of the LORD blocks the road; the donkey sees the angel but Balaam does not. Three times the donkey stops and Balaam punishes her, and suddenly the donkey begins to speak, criticizing Balaam's behavior toward her. Then, just as "the LORD opened the mouth of the donkey" (v. 28) so also the LORD "opens the eyes of Balaam" (v. 31) so that he sees the angel. Balaam offers to go back home. The angel, however, tells him to continue his journey, but to speak only God's word. Abruptly the story is back to the narrative starting point of vv. 20-21, before this entire incident of the donkey and the angel.

This story of the talking donkey is surely one of the great vignettes of the OT, unusual for its colorful detail. Surely the reader is meant to let out a hearty laugh as the tale is told. The most stubborn and unintelligent, the most maligned of animals (at least in postbiblical Western tradition) sees what the great seer does not. Balaam's specialty is seeing, divining, seeking omens, gaining contact with the world of the gods; he is regarded as the best in the world in this profession. Yet he sees no angel, blames the donkey for making his journey difficult, wants to kill the donkey . . . until God opens the donkey's mouth for a conversation that prepares the way for the opening of Balaam's eyes.

What does this incident contribute theologically? The donkey story modifies and enhances the overall story of the emissaries and Balaam. Balaam may secretly have been hoping that God's mind had changed, for God's second response (v. 20) did not repeat the specific information that Israel was blessed. Of course, God's mind has not changed. Thus God must get Balaam's attention through the angel to reemphasize Balaam's duty to speak only God's word. In this experience Balaam begins to discover that there is no turning back. He will not be able to avoid a confrontation with Balak. He might never have had to deal with the tension between being paid and speaking truth if he had listened to God's first word to him and not asked again.

Whether the command to go in God's second word was really meant as a command or whether it was a test cannot be determined with certainty. Commentators are divided on this point. But once Balaam is underway, for whatever reason, God wants him to be clear, and absolutely clear, that he will speak God's word and nothing else. The alternative of avoiding the situation is no longer possible. Balaam's proposal to turn back is countered by the angel's command to continue with the emissaries of Balak. At this point, Balaam finally understands what lies ahead. And now the narrator has put the readers fully on notice of the ending of the story. Balaam, reputedly the most effective curse-or-blessing pronouncer in the ancient world, will speak blessing on Israel whom God has declared blessed. God will use Balaam to make clear to King Balak and to all who later hear this story that Israel is blessed with a blessing that cannot be countermanded.

The narrative introduces the role of the angel as that of "adversary" (NRSV) to Balaam (vv. 22, 32). Behind the term "adversary" lies the Hebrew word *satan*. Obviously this is not the Satan figure of later biblical thought, since here in Numbers the angel is precisely representing God as adversary of Balaam, rather than acting in opposition to God. The early general meaning of the term as "adversary" (e.g., David as "adversary" to the Philistines, 1 Sam. 29:4) is present here; it is only late in the postexilic era that the term becomes restricted to a specific demonic being in adversarial relationship to God.

Many modern readers, especially in Western cultures, find the story either quaint or uncomfortable. They are not accustomed to talking animals as a way God uses to get people's attention. Such readers are also uncomfortable with many other OT stories about God's encounters with human beings. These encounters include burning bushes (Moses), rushing wind (Job), heavenly seraphs carrying coals (Isaiah), other angels with or without swords (Joshua, Samson's mother, Hagar). But when readers (ancient or modern) laugh at Balaam, it is not just because God's means are so odd; rather it is because Balaam is so obtuse, because he has such a hard time getting the message. Therein lies another point of the story for readers of every generation who believe that they have heard God's message rightly, yet suppose that nothing will be required of them. Balaam's story stands as a reminder that God does use improbable means to set people on improbable paths. This is especially true of people who are called to enact blessing upon those whom the world wants cursed.

22:36-41   and subsequent prose of chapters 23–24 The travellers are met by King Balak at the most distant point of the Moabite border; but the king's opening words are only a complaint that Balaam had not come sooner. Balaam informs him that although he has come he will be able to speak only "the word God puts in [his] mouth" (Num. 22:38).

Like a long theological prologue, the narrative of ch. 22 has made claims for the power of God, the effectiveness of Balaam, and the intent of God to bless Israel. Now at last those claims are to be tested through the series of Balaam's oracles in response to Balak's desire that he curse Israel. Despite the preceding expectation of a positive result for Israel, tension remains. What exactly will Balaam say? Will he try to resist the divine word? The sequence of oracles is presented in chs. 22–24. Four prose units (22:41–23:7; 23:11-18; 23:25–24:3; 24:10-14) introduce Balaam's four oracles. In the first two rounds altars are built and sacrifices prepared; Balaam goes aside to seek God's word; he receives a word from God, and utters the oracle. As the reader has been led to expect, all of the results are oracles of blessing, not curses. After the first round, King Balak complains and Balaam reiterates a theme of ch. 22, saying, "Must I not take care to say what the LORD puts into my mouth?" (23:12). Balak suggests that they try again from a different location, where Balaam cannot see all of the Israelites. This change of location does not change the result, and King Balak suggests that if Balaam cannot curse the people he at least should refrain from blessing them. Balaam replies, "Whatever the LORD says, that is what I must do" (23:25-26).

Balak proposes yet a third location, and again altars and sacrifices are prepared. On this third occasion, however, Balaam does not go aside to seek a word from the LORD as he had done previously. It is reported that he did not "look for omens" because he "saw that it pleased the LORD to bless Israel" (24:1). In fact, the phrase "look for omens" is a new expression used here; in the first two rounds, Balaam says he will go aside to "meet the LORD" (23:3, 15). The text does not explain Balaam's motive in not going aside. Overtly, he recognizes God's unchangeable power to bless, as expressed in his first oracle (23:8), and so has no need to inquire what he should say on this third occasion. Yet it is possible that he may secretly hope that by not consulting the deity he will be able to speak a curse and earn his pay. This ambiguity may be a source or reinforcement of the NT tradition that Balaam sought to earn a profit by cursing Israel. In any case, "the spirit of God [comes] upon him" (24:2), and yet another oracle of blessing results.

After this third oracle of blessing Balak orders Balaam to leave without pay. Balaam replies that he had said from the start that regardless of pay, . . . "I would not be able to go beyond the word of the LORD . . ." (24:13). Before departing, Balaam volunteers yet a fourth oracle, predicting the future domination of Israel over its neighbors, including Moab. The introductory lines of the fourth oracle indicate that it, like those preceding, is from God; but the divine origin of this oracle is not made explicit in its prose introduction. The story concludes with the brief notice that Balaam went home (24:25).

One purpose for preserving the Balaam narrative was of course to provide a context for the ancient poems of chs. 23–24 announcing God's special relationship to Israel and predicting Israel's glorious future. But the narrative material just reviewed raises several important theological issues in its own right.

A primary concern is how one should live as a person paid to bless or curse others. In general any paid attempts, under human auspices, to know the future or to affect the course of the future were unacceptable in Israel (e.g., Lev. 19:26, 31; 20:27; Deut. 18:10-11; 1 Sam. 28:3ff.). Perhaps the NT criticism of Balaam reads one side of the story correctly in assuming he went to Balak knowing that he would be paid only for cursing Israel and therefore hoping that he could do so. This is possible, even though he kept emphasizing that he would say only what God permitted.

Israel surely recognized this tension between divine truth and human intentions in its own experience. There was a long-standing tradition of prophets who were related to the royal court. These prophets constantly faced the tension between what the king wanted to hear and what God required them to say. Kings were permitted and expected to inquire of these prophets. Some, like Nathan, were part of the official court, as if on the payroll. Although the role of such prophets focused on proclaiming God's future, that future involved either weal or woe, blessing or disaster for those of whom, and to whom, they spoke. Those prophets who spoke an unpopular word could be put to death (Jer. 26:20-23) or at least be banished from the court (see Micaiah, 1 Kgs. 22:26-27). Since these prophetic figures were Israelite, their troubles came from speaking negatively of Israel's future. In the Balaam story, the *foreign* king rejects God's spokesperson for *blessing* Israel. This brings into sharp focus the reversed situation of these Israelite prophets, whom the *Israelite* kings rejected because they announced God's *judgment* upon Israel.

Did Balaam have a choice about speaking the word of God? At some points it appears that the central issue of the story is obedience. God commands Balaam to speak only what God tells him to say, and only through Balaam's perfect obedience will King Balak be challenged and Israel be blessed (e.g., Num. 22:20, 35). On the other hand, other places in the narrative suggest that Balaam has no choice in the matter. The seer is simply the vehicle for uttering the word that God wants uttered, and so he "must" speak óracles of blessing (e.g., 22:38). In yet other places, it is impossible to determine from the Hebrew which emphasis is intended (e.g., 23:5, 12). Through this ambiguity the narrator has accomplished something theologically remarkable: the story refuses to decide whether Balaam spoke freely or whether he was compelled by God. This deliberate ambiguity about how and why Balaam spoke God's word describes the experience of generations of Israel's prophets (see Amos 7; Jer. 20). The same tension between compelling force and free decision is also important in many Christian traditions as one criterion for identifying a valid call to church leadership.

CHAPTERS 23 AND 24
(POETRY SECTIONS)

These chapters present the four oracles of Balaam. The prose sections surrounding these four oracles have been discussed in connection with the preceding narrative of Num. 22.

A review of the content of the four oracles shows that the first two speak directly of Balaam and Balak and therefore require the prose narrative context for understanding. Oracles three and four, however, are general in scope, with no reference to the narrative in which they are embedded. Some scholars therefore propose different origins for the two pairs of oracles. Generally they suggest that three and four were older, independent poems of blessing that were incorporated into the story. It is proposed that oracles one and two were created especially for the story, perhaps in imitation of three and four.

The date of composition of the oracles has also been much discussed; many scholars today look to the period of the early monarchy as a likely context, but debate continues. This debate is occasioned partly by the numerous textual difficulties in the oracles that make translation uncertain. Difficulty in determining the referents of poetic allusions further compounds the challenge of interpreting these poems. The interested reader may pursue these issues in more technical commentaries (e.g., Martin Noth, Jules de Vaulx, Philip Budd; see bibliography).

23:7-10 Numbers 23:7-9a summarize the narrative and the problem Balaam faces in trying to fulfill his paid commission in the face of a different divine intention. In v. 9b Israel's people-hood is contrasted with the nation-state status of those around about, suggesting both Israel's premonarchical condition and possibly its special relationship with God. The "dust of Jacob" (v. 10a) refers to the great number of the Israelites, which has of course frightened King Balak (22:3-5). Here the comparison to dust suggests the fulfillment of God's promise of blessing to Abraham in the form of many progeny (cf. Gen. 13:16; 28:14), so that God's blessing of Israel is spoken of as something already accomplished. The oracle concludes with Balaam's hope that he may meet a fate like Israel's (Num. 23:10b). This hope may be connected to the promise of God's blessing to those who bless Israel (Gen. 12:3), as well as the promise of blessing to others through Israel (Gen. 12:3; 28:14).

23:18-24 Again the content of the oracle is related to the tension between Balak's commission to Balaam and God's plan for Israel. God's mind will not be changed because of Balak's wishes, and the power of God's uttered word will bring its effect into being (Num. 23:19). In the face of God's constancy and effective word, Balaam can do nothing other than bless Israel (v. 20). No trouble will befall Israel because the God Yahweh whom Israel calls King, who brings them out of Egypt, is with them (vv. 21-22). The reference to "the horns of a wild ox" is obscure. Syntactically the Hebrew expression may refer to God (as translated in the NRSV) or to Israel. Because of God's power, manifest in Israel, no divination is possible against the people (v. 23). Israel will achieve its destiny like a hungry lion or lioness (v. 24). Comparison of individual tribes to a lion occurs in Gen. 49:9 and Deut. 33:20, both in poems blessing the tribes of Israel.

24:3-9 The third oracle opens with the poetic assertion that Balaam's words are given to him by God (Num. 24:3-4). "Almighty" (v. 4; Hebrew *Shaddai*) is an ancient name for the God of Israel. The beauty of Israel's encampment is compared to gardens or groves of trees close to life-giving water (vv. 5-6). The translation of v. 7a is difficult, although an image of fruitfulness for Israel's life seems clear. Agag (v. 7b) was a king of the Amalekites who was defeated in the time of Saul (1 Sam. 15); the Amalekites were a wilderness enemy of Israel (Exod. 17:8-16). Numbers 24:8-9a reiterates themes of 23:22-24, and 24:9b (cf.

Gen. 12:3) is a more forthright expression of the theme of 23:10b.

24:15-24   This fourth and final poetic section is made up of four shorter oracles. The first concerning Israel (24:15-19) is followed by three brief words concerning other peoples.

The oracle concerning Israel opens (vv. 15-16) in the same way as the previous one (cf. vv. 3-4). Balaam then speaks of a future figure, evidently royal (v. 17a), who will gain control over Moab and its neighboring territories to the south (vv. 17b-19). Most commentators interpret this section as a reference to King David and his military control of that region. In later Christian tradition the mention of star and scepter led to appropriation of the text to refer to Christ's reign.

The first of the additional words concerns the perishing of the Amalekites (v. 20). It may pick up on the reference to Agag in v. 7.

The next oracle envisages affliction of the Kenites at the hands of Asshur (vv. 21-22). The Kenites are spoken of variously in biblical tradition. They are remembered as a subgroup of the Midianites who were thus indirectly related to the Israelites (see, e.g., 10:29; Judg. 4:11). From about 1200 B.C.E. on into the time of the Israelite monarchy, the Kenites appear to have lived in the area southeast of Arad. If the reference to Asshur means Assyria, then the context may be the eighth century, when Assyria was asserting control over Israel and Judah.

The final oracle (Num. 24:23-24) is quite obscure. No one group is identified as the subject. Kittim in biblical tradition usually means Cyprus. Asshur cannot be certainly identified. It may refer to Assyria, or to some ancient tribe, or even to the Seleucid dynasty of the third to second centuries B.C.E. The meaning of Eber is uncertain. It is only clear that "affliction" is envisaged.

What is the theological import of these oracles of Balaam as a whole? These oracles, especially as they are set in their narrative context, place Israel's future not in the hands of the king of Moab, but rather in the hands of the God of Israel. The point is not so

133

obvious or so self-evident as it may seem. Despite the history of disobedience of the generation of Israelites that left Egypt, God is determined to bless this people. Surely the significance of this basic theme was experienced differently by the faith community in different periods of Israel's history. During the time of David and Solomon, when Israel's hegemony stretched to its maximum over the surrounding nations (including Moab), oracles such as these declared Israel's glorious destiny as Yahweh's people. Later in the monarchical period, however, the significance of such oracles must have been much disputed. Prophets came to announce that the Day of the LORD would be "darkness, not light" (Amos 5:20), judgment and destruction, not blessing and prosperity.

What happens when a people destined for blessing turns its back on God? The OT answer, indeed the biblical answer, to this question is that God's mercy always outlives God's wrath. The relationship between God and people is never finally broken. Yet the scripture as a whole, OT and NT alike, also bears witness that blessing is meant particularly for those who are weak, who are needy, who seek to do justice and to love mercy and to walk attentively with God. Balak was afraid of Israel because he saw that they had "spread over the face of the earth" (Num. 22:5). What Balak did not realize was that their power lay not in any numerical strength but in the presence of God with them. As the wilderness era ends and the people stand near the Jordan River, the story of Balaam and King Balak re-echoes the theological claim made at the beginning of the Exodus saga, in the story of Pharaoh's effort to destroy the Israelite infants. No enemy, no earthly power, no Egyptian Pharaoh or Moabite King, can ultimately thwart God's will to bless God's people.

Yet Israel has no active role in this Balaam story. Indeed, Israel is totally unaware of these unfolding events. From the time of Israel's slavery in Egypt and throughout the wilderness era, the people had cried out to God, sometimes for good reason but often without justification. They were always living in fear of disaster — death of their children, bricks without straw, no food, no water, enemies, disappearing leaders, and on and on. In the Balaam story the Israelites are potentially in much more serious trouble (words of cursing are powerful), but they are not even aware of it. Only the readers of the story are privy to Balak's plot and Balaam's role. Here God protects Israel even when Israel does not know enough to realize that it is in need of protection. Blessing is extended and maintained before it is asked for or even known to be needed. The story of Balaam bears witness to God's power and God's grace at work even before the needy cry out for help.

CHAPTER 25

At Shittim, a place further specifying Israel's location on the plains of Moab, the people engage in an act of extreme apostasy. They bow down to the god called Baal of Peor. The story is of Israelite men engaging in sexual activity and worship with Moabite (25:1) and Midianite (vv. 6, 14ff.) women. This reference to two foreign peoples, coupled with the fact that neither God's directive (v. 4) nor Moses' directive (v. 5) is carried out in the story, has led scholars to the supposition that two or more versions of the story have been conflated here. As Jacob Milgrom points out, however, this same pattern of Midianite individuals appearing in a Moabite story appears in 22:4, 7; and it is possible to understand that some Midianites lived under Moabite hegemony (Milgrom, *Numbers*, 185, 476-77). Despite the tensions, therefore, it is possible to appreciate the received narrative as a literary unit.

25:1-5 The precise content of the apostasy is disputed, since it is not clear in what way the sexual relations were related to the worship of the god Baal of Peor. Ritual sexual activity as part of a fertility rite has often been proposed. There is no clear evidence, however, that human beings ever ritually reenacted the sexual encounters of male and female deities known from ancient mythological texts. Sexual activity has also been supposed to belong to religious rites relating to worship of the dead, but again the evidence is not secure and the relation to this passage is uncertain at best. Quite possibly engaging in ordinary sexual activity with foreign women led the Israelite men to participate in non-Israelite worship. It should be noted that the opening verses do not specify how the sexual liaisons began; it is only at the very end of the

136

narrative (25:16-18) that the foreigners are held at fault, a theme
that will be lifted up again in ch. 31.   .

God is angered and instructs Moses to impale all the chiefs of
the people to appease this divine anger. Impaling is rare in the
OT; in Israel and in the ancient Near East this form of execution
seems to be especially associated with expiation for wrongdoing.
Oddly, Moses says nothing about this command from God and
takes no action. Instead, he orders the judges to put to death
those who personally participated in the apostasy.

25:6-9 Before any action is taken Moses and the people are
weeping "at the entrance of the tent of meeting," that is, in the
presence of God. While this is taking place, an Israelite man brings
a Midianite woman to his tent. Phinehas, a grandson of Aaron,
goes to that tent and pierces the couple through, apparently as
they are having sex. Phinehas' action brings a halt to a plague in
which twenty-four thousand people died. This plague is presumably a consequence of God's anger, but it has not previously
been mentioned. Neither Moses nor the judges take any action
on the instructions given to them. The effective action of Phinehas
seems to fall far short of the mass executions commanded in
25:4-5. A note at the end of the story, however, reveals that the
couple killed by Phinehas were highly placed leaders (vv. 14-15);
perhaps their rank is intended to explain the sufficiency of his
action (see below). Later Jewish tradition was concerned that
Phinehas created a bad precedent by taking the law into his own
hands; his action was excused as a special case because of his
genuine zeal for God (Milgrom, *Numbers,* 215). Despite its tensions, this received form of the story sets the stage for the remainder of the chapter.

25:10-13 God offers a covenant to Phinehas and to his descendants, granting to them "perpetual priesthood" because of
his atoning action on behalf of Israel. This promise provides the
theological rationale for the special privileges of the Zadokite
priestly line (Phinehas' descendants) for service in the temple.
This is in contrast to the line of Abiathar that was dismissed from
temple service in the reign of Solomon (1 Kgs. 2:26-27). (See

the Introduction for a discussion of the problems of reconstructing the history of priesthood in Israel.)

The framework of the Pentateuch as a whole is constructed partly around a series of covenants, representing different eras in the history of the world and of Israel. The first is the covenant with Noah, with the promise that God will never again destroy the earth by flood (Gen. 9). There follows a covenant with Abraham, promising that he and his descendants will have land and numerous offspring, and that the other nations will find blessing through this people. This Abrahamic covenant is made explicit in Gen. 15; the promise theme appears repeatedly beginning in Gen. 12. A third covenant is related to the experience of Abraham's descendants at Mt. Sinai. There, through the giving of the law, they are established as a sacral community with established forms of worship and communal organization.

God's covenant with Phinehas does not appear to be directly related to the structured sequence of pentateuchal covenants. It is more readily compared to God's promise of perpetuity to the Davidic royal line (Ps. 89; 2 Sam. 23:5; 2 Sam. 7, although the term "covenant" does not appear in this passage). Through these covenants with David and Phinehas, God's plan for political and cultic leadership is interpreted to the community. Each covenant serves not only to establish a given line, but also in effect to disestablish a competing claim. (Both the priestly line of Abiathar and the whole sequence of kings from the northern kingdom are discredited in this way.) These dissenting claims are criticized and rejected by the final form of the OT. Even so, they serve as a reminder that God's will was not always obvious in the time of the events recorded in Scripture. The points of view affirmed by the canon represent for the most part the views of those groups who prevailed in the debates within the community.

25:14-15   The names of the couple killed by Phinehas are given as Zimri, son of Salu, and Cozbi, daughter of Zur. Both are of high rank (as heir to the head of an Israelite ancestral house and daughter of a comparable Midianite clan head). This lends at least a symbolic level of fulfilment to the command of God that chiefs of the people should die, as well as to Moses' word that perpetrators should be put to death.

25:16-17   God's command to defeat Midian provides an anticipatory connection to the command that opens Num. 31 and to the rationale for the slaughter given in 31:16.

CENSUS OF THE
NEW GENERATION
(26:1-65)

records

CHAPTER 26

God instructs Moses and Eleazar to take a census. This second census, like the one recorded in ch. 1, is a count by tribes of the males age twenty and up. Levi is counted separately (26:57-62), in parallel to 3:14-20.

The phrase "who came out of the land of Egypt" (26:4b) might suggest that this census is simply an updating of records. The conclusion of the chapter, however, makes clear that this is in fact a census of the new generation of adult males (vv. 63-65). Of the original Israelite adult males, only Joshua, Caleb, and of course Moses are still left alive. Those counted here are any males who were under age twenty at the time of the original census, plus any males born in the wilderness who have at this point reached age twenty or above. The tacit presumption may be that the adult women who left Egypt have also died during the forty years. This point, though, is not of interest to the census tradition.

Verses 63-65 are clearly connected to the story of rebellion against taking the land in ch. 14. This, combined with the location "in the plains of Moab" (26:3), confirms the watershed importance of this second census. From now on the story deals only with those who were under age twenty or not yet born in the time of the unfaithful spies. This is the listing of the generation that will in fact enter the land. The critical importance of this change of generations is seen in the overall structure of the narrative: there are no more stories of murmuring or disobedience after this point. The new generation will be portrayed as perfectly obedient, even as the old generation has been portrayed as constantly rebellious (Olson, *The Death of the Old*).

26:1-51 Verses 1-4 give instructions for taking the census; the results of the census are reported in vv. 5-51. Although the order of listing of the tribes is the same as in ch. 1 except for the reversal of Ephraim and Manasseh, additional material is supplied concerning clan names. These names generally conform to those given in Gen. 46, although the order of tribes is different there; the precise character of the relationship between the two texts is not clear. The connection between these two texts does account, however, for the notice about the deaths of Er and Onan (Num. 26:19; cf. Gen. 46:12) who were never part of the wilderness group.

Compared to the first census, there are significant differences in the numbers attributed to various individual tribes. Nevertheless, the numerical total of the second generation is nearly identical to that counted in the first census. There is a reduction of less than two thousand male adults, from 603,550 to 601,730. Whatever the origin of the numbers on a tribe-by-tribe basis, and however these numbers are to be reckoned (see commentary on Num. 1), the consistency of the totals makes an important theological point. Through God's guiding care this people has been preserved as a people, despite the dangers of the wilderness, and despite their fickle behavior and lapses of faith.

The census also incorporates two additional notes concerning certain groups and individuals during the wilderness period. First, the story of the rebellion of Dathan and Abiram and the company of Korah is called to mind (26:9-11; cf. ch. 16) within the report of the Reubenite clans. Second, it is noted that the Manassite Zelophehad had no sons, but only daughters (26:33). Both of these comments are included in anticipation of the narrative of ch. 27.

26:52-56 God instructs Moses concerning the purpose for this second census. It is to serve as the basis for land distribution. Larger tribes are to receive proportionately larger territories (26:54). This numerical principle is modified, however, by a separate principle that apparently concerns location; the land is to be "apportioned by lot" (v. 55). The exact procedure for combining these two principles is not made clear. It seems sensible to suppose that general regions were to be determined by casting lots, while specific borders would be drawn to take account of relative numbers of people (cf. 33:54; 34:13).

26:57-62   Although no specific command is given from God, this census of the Levites completes the task of numbering all the people. Their census is separate, as in the opening chapters, because they are not to be landholders and thus are enumerated outside the formal count of twelve tribes. The enrollment begins at the age of one month (26:62), thus conforming to the pattern of 3:15-16. The reference to the death of Nadab and Abihu corresponds to 3:2-4 (cf. Lev. 10:1-3) and explains why no descendants of theirs are numbered. No special purpose is stated for the numbering of the Levites.

Various problems of technical interest are raised by these few verses. Perhaps the most conspicuous is in Num. 26:58a. The five Levitical clans mentioned here are otherwise unknown, and they seem to stand in unresolved relationship with the familiar list of three (Gershon, Kohath, and Merari) listed in v. 57. Whether these five represent some subdivision of the original three or whether they are some fragmentary recollection of forgotten clans cannot be determined.

26:63-65   As indicated in the introductory comments about the chapter, this summarizing section corrects any possible misunderstanding of v. 4b. In so doing it also establishes the importance of the second census as a turning point in the literary structure of the book of Numbers.

MISCELLANEOUS LEGISLATION; EVENTS PRIOR TO MOSES' DEATH (27:1–36:13)

CHAPTER 27

The chapter reports two events: an appeal concerning inheritance laws and the investiture of Joshua as Moses' successor.

27:1-11 These verses present the first part of the story of Zelophehad's daughters; the second part of the story forms the conclusion to the book of Numbers in ch. 36. The daughters' names are Mahlah, Noah, Hoglah, Milcah, and Tirzah. Since so many women mentioned in the OT are known only as daughter or wife of a certain named male, it is noteworthy that the names of these five women are listed in full not only here but also in 26:33; 36:11; and Josh. 17:3.

The daughters of Zelophehad approach Moses to request that since their father had died having no sons they be allowed to receive a possession of land that would ordinarily have been received by male offspring (Num. 27:1-4). The women note that their father had died "for his own sin," and was not a part of Korah's rebellion (v. 3; cf. ch. 16). Therefore, there is no taint attached to their clan that would differentiate it from the others who are to inherit. Moses inquires of God, who rules in favor of the daughters' request (27:5-7). A generalized law concerning sequence of inheritance is then promulgated as an appendix to the specific case (vv. 8-11).

The narrative portrays women of great initiative. As unmarried women whose father has died, they have little or no power or standing in the Israelite community. Perhaps they show the boldness of those who have nothing to lose; yet their action is no less remarkable. They dare to challenge God's own spokesperson Moses and implicitly to suggest that God's own decrees given through Moses may have overlooked an important point. Other biblical narratives of appeals for justice are usually based on what is already known of God's will, rather than presenting a challenge suggesting the incompleteness or inadequacy of God's law. The event takes place in the most public arena possible, at the entrance to the tent of meeting. The women speak their concern not only before Moses, but also before Eleazar, the leaders, and the entire congregation.

Although the narrative heightens the drama of the women's action, its focal concern is a problem faced by male members of a patrilineal culture. The story addresses the structural concern of a male-oriented society and the anxiety of individual men about the consequences of fathering no sons, but only daughters. In a context of tribal allotments where preservation of name and possession of land are tied together, the narrator places this societal concern into the mouth of the daughters: "Why should the name of our father be taken away from his clan because he had no son? Give us a possession . . ." (v. 4). The narrative does not offer any clue whether the five daughters themselves believed in this rationale for their request, or whether it was a matter of strategic convenience in presenting their case. It is reasonable to suppose that the (male) narrator imagines that the daughters concur in his assumption of this cultural perspective. The story may be read at one level as a story of comfort for women who will not be left destitute in the Israelite social structure. At another level, however, it is a story of comfort for men who have the misfortune not to bear male heirs. Their names will not be lost from the roster of Israel.

Since the narrative incorporates no word of the daughters' response to Moses' pronouncement from God, the focus on the women and their particular interest are lost in the shift to the general case law concerning inheritance. Case law probably developed into codified form much more gradually than this story suggests, probably village by village and region by region. Even so, the text does illustrate the way in which discussion of circumstances not covered by existing tradition might be dealt with in a community setting.

The story raises tantalizing questions about the place of women in Israelite society. However, the lack of adequate corroborating evidence and also the likelihood of variations over time and region make firm answers to these questions impossible. It might be inferred from this story, for instance, that ordinary women were permitted direct access to the male authority structure to make appeal in their own right, without the necessity of a man to make the appeal for them. Was such direct access by women the norm? Or was it an exception permitted to women whose circumstances left them with no male in direct authority over them? Or was the direct appeal of these women to Moses in violation of all the norms of their society? The story of the two women who appeared before Solomon with their dispute over motherhood of an infant raises the same questions (1 Kgs. 3:16-28). Direct access even by an ordinary man to figures of the stature of Solomon or Moses was presumably very exceptional; these stories heighten the unusual by presenting women in the role of petitioner, but the nuances of what is unusual cannot be determined with certainty.

The text also suggests that women were able to inherit and possess property under limited and prescribed circumstances. (Additional limitations are specified in Num. 36.) This assumption that women did occasionally hold land presumes that the legislation of 27:8-11 was actually in effect at some time, not just an ideal that never gained acceptance in the community. Evidence is insufficient to know how often women may have held land, or whether there were any other means by which women might have gained control of land.

27:12-23   God instructs Moses to go to a mountaintop to view the Promised Land before his death. God mentions again the sin that has prevented Moses and Aaron from leading the people into the land. Moses does not carry out God's instruction to go to the mountaintop (see below). Rather, Moses responds by expressing his concern for the future leadership of the people. The image of shepherd for human leadership (v. 17) is attested throughout the OT (cf. esp. 1 Kgs. 22:17) and in the ancient Near East. Two technical Hebrew expressions are used here: to "go out and come in" before the people and to "lead them out and bring them in." Each of these expressions is used elsewhere to indicate the full range of leadership responsibilities (e.g., 1 Kgs. 3:7). Sometimes these phrases are specifically associated with military leadership, for which Joshua as Moses' successor will later become famous. For example, David's military leadership causes the northern tribes to acclaim him as "shepherd" and anoint him as king (2 Sam. 5:2). Here in Numbers the phrases probably refer to a whole range of leadership skills, but with particular focus on military leadership.

God then instructs Moses to commission Joshua, describing the future leader as already spirit-imbued (Num. 27:18). The precise meaning or effect of this "spirit" in Joshua is not further defined. Its presence, however, indicates that Joshua already has the quality or qualification for the leadership role he is being given. The laying on of Moses' hands will invest him with some of Moses' "authority" (NRSV), but it will not make him a different person. The term translated "authority" (Hebrew *hod*) is elsewhere more usually translated "splendor" or "majesty," often referring either to God or to a king. Understanding "authority" in this larger frame of reference helps to clarify why only a portion of Moses' authority is to be placed upon Joshua. Moses' unique leadership role is carefully maintained.

The commissioning takes place, as God has instructed, in the presence of Eleazar and the congregation by the laying on of hands. Joshua receives a portion of Moses' authority and is to heed Eleazar's use of the Urim. The Urim are thought to be a pair of marked stones used to obtain yes-or-no advice concerning a question. Similar objects remain in use in many cultures today.

Deuteronomy 32:48-52 offers a parallel version of the instruction to Moses in Num. 27:12 to go to a mountaintop in anticipation of his death. The Deuteronomy text introduces greater geographic specification, including mention of Mt. Nebo. Moses' trip to the mountaintop is finally recorded in Deut. 34, after his farewell blessing of the people (Deut. 33). Various redactional and literary theories attempt to explain why instruction about Moses' death has been included in Num. 27, so far before his actual death. Since most scholars believe that Deuteronomy circulated as a separate document before being combined with the first four books of the Pentateuch, it is possible that the story of the first four books once ended here, with the report of Moses' death following immediately upon the commissioning of Joshua. Naturally the story of Moses' death had to be moved to the end of Deuteronomy once the books were combined. Since God's instruction to Moses to prepare for death occasions Moses' request to commission his successor, that portion of the story was retained here. According to this analysis, the remaining material of the book of Numbers is regarded as a series of late appendixes.

On the other hand, the narratives of chs. 31–32 do seem thoroughly linked to Moses and quite possibly older than the joining of Deuteronomy to the other books. Thus, others approach the problem of the location of 27:12-23 from a different point of view, focusing upon what role the commissioning of Joshua plays at this point in the received form of the tradition. The introduction of Joshua here fits well with the immediately preceding context. Chapter 26 has drawn attention to the future in the land in three ways: the people who will cross the Jordan under Joshua have been counted; God has given instruction concerning the division of the land, instructions that will be carried out by Joshua (Josh. 14:1); and it has been recalled that Caleb and Joshua alone of the old generation will enter the land — indeed, Joshua's name is the concluding word of ch. 26. The beginning of ch. 27 follows directly upon ch. 26 in providing a detail concerning the future land distribution. Thus the establishment of Joshua as future leader of Israel in 27:12-23 is a reasonable next step in the literary sequence.

The introductory instruction concerning Moses' death in fact serves to highlight the close connection between the commissioning of Joshua and the commissioning of Eleazar (20:22-29). The parallel between the two commissionings is established by the close parallels between the narrative of the death of Aaron (20:24-29) and the anticipated death of Moses (27:13). In ch. 20 Aaron is called to a mountaintop to die, and his death is tied to his joint rebellion with Moses ("you [plural] rebelled," 20:24). In that context Eleazar is established as Aaron's successor. So also in ch. 27, Moses' final trip to a mountaintop is tied to his joint rebellion with Aaron ("you [plural] rebelled," 27:14); in this context Joshua is established as Moses' successor.

Some of Moses' authority is imparted to Joshua (v. 20). Although Joshua is already a person of spirit (v. 18), the relationship
between Joshua and Eleazar is not to be the same as that between
Moses and Aaron (see commentary on ch. 20). Whereas Moses
is slightly more powerful than Aaron in what is presented narra-
tively as close to a parity relationship, this pattern appears to be
reversed in the next generation. The decisions of God will not
be revealed to Joshua directly, but only through Eleazar's use of
the Urim (27:20-21). This state of affairs guards the authority of
the priesthood, especially for the postexilic era after the decline
of prophecy. At the same time it guards for all time the unique
authority of Moses, with whom alone the LORD spoke "face to
face" (12:8).

CHAPTER 28

This chapter and the one following provide a summary of the required schedule of burnt offerings in an annual cycle, together with other required accompanying offerings. The summary begins with daily requirements, then moves to weekly and monthly additions, and finally to additions for the religious festival cycle of the Israelite year. Most specialists in the history of Israel's worship believe that the full requirements of these two chapters represent worship practice during the postexilic Second Temple period. Which parts of what is required here were carried out in earlier times is very difficult to ascertain. Other instructions about sacrifice that differ in details from Num. 28–29 are found in various other parts of Exodus through Deuteronomy. Indeed, nearly all of Israel's recorded cultic instruction is placed at the very beginning of Israel's life as a worshipping community, so that it has the imprimatur of God's revelation through Moses.

28:1-8 The daily offering consists of two lambs, one to be offered in the morning, the other at twilight. The lambs here and elsewhere throughout the subsequent regulations must be males, one year old, and without blemish. Each lamb is to be accompanied by a grain offering of flour mixed with oil and by a drink offering of an alcoholic brew. Many scholars believe that the Hebrew term translated "strong drink" in the NRSV means a kind of beer. The amount of accompanying offering is identical morning and evening.

28:9-10 The sabbath day offering is in addition to the regular offerings specified in 28:1-8. It consists of two lambs, with ac-

155

companying grain and drink offerings in the same proportion per animal as specified in vv. 1-8.

28:11-15   At the beginning of each month further additional offerings are required: two young bulls, one ram, and seven lambs. The volume of the accompanying offerings remains the same per lamb; the grain offering is tripled for each bull and doubled for the ram, and the drink offerings are also larger. In addition, a male goat is used as a sin offering.

28:16-25   This section concerns special offerings for the first-month festival of Passover and Unleavened Bread. Initially there is a Passover offering on the fourteenth of the month. The content of the sacrifice is not specified in this text; it is described in Exod. 12:1-13. This is followed by an offering to be made on the fifteenth day of the month. The animals and accompanying grain offering are the same as those specified for the beginning of months (Num. 28:11-15). The fifteenth day inaugurates a seven-day period of eating unleavened bread. The people are instructed to hold a "holy convocation" (vv. 18, 25) once at the beginning and again at the end of this period. This technical term apparently refers to a festival occasion on which ordinary work is not to be done. The notice that the burnt offerings shall be repeated daily for seven days (v. 24) incorporates mention of the accompanying drink offering.

28:26-31   The offering for the Firstfruits festival, also called the Festival of Weeks, is specified. The time of this festival is not specified, but other texts (esp. Lev. 23:15-21) make clear that it follows fifty days after the Feast of Unleavened Bread. The festival itself involves a grain offering and a day of holy convocation without work. Once again the burnt offering and its accompanying offerings are to be the same as those required for the beginning of months (Num. 28:11-15). As in the previous section, the drink offering is mentioned only in passing in the summation (v. 31).

CHAPTER 29

This chapter continues the instructions concerning burnt offerings that begin in ch. 28. Chapter 29 is concerned entirely with festival observances during the seventh month.

29:1-6 The first day of the seventh month requires a holy convocation, with no regular work and with the blowing of trumpets. The burnt offering is to consist of one bull, one ram, and seven lambs. The accompanying grain offering is in the same proportions per animal as throughout ch. 28. It is reiterated (29:6) that these offerings are in addition to the regular daily and monthly burnt offerings with their accompanying grain and drink offerings. The text does not specify any additional drink offering for this occasion.

29:7-11 The tenth day offering repeats the specifications for the first day of this month. Almost in passing, the sin offering for atonement (v. 11; cf. Lev. 23:26-32) is mentioned as a feature of this month.

29:12-16 On the fifteenth day, again a holy convocation day, a much larger offering is required: thirteen bulls, two rams, fourteen lambs. Again the proportions of the accompanying grain offering are the same per animal; again these are in addition to the regular daily offerings. This is the first day of the Festival of Booths (also called Tabernacles, or Succoth), which is described more briefly in Lev. 23:33-36.

29:17-38 The offerings for each of the subsequent days of the

Festival of Booths are outlined. Each day the number of rams and lambs remains the same as on the first day. The number of bulls decreases by one per day, until on the seventh day seven bulls are offered (Num. 29:32). Here the accompanying drink offerings clearly reappear alongside the grain offerings, to be presented in prescribed proportion to the number of each type of animal. The presentation of the drink offerings throughout the annual festival materials is inconsistent. This suggests that these offerings may be a later addition to the sacrificial requirements, which has not been consistently incorporated into the written regulations.

The eighth day of the festival marks its conclusion; this should be on the twenty-second day of the month. The specified offering is the same as for the first day of the seventh month (vv. 2-5).

29:39-40   These verses are a summarizing conclusion. They remind Israel that votive and freewill offerings are not included in the list of the preceding two chapters.

Scholars are unable to reconstruct the changing details of observance of these numerous daily, periodic, and festival sacrifices and offerings over the more than one thousand years of worship in the First and Second Temple periods. Apparently many of the practices recorded in Num. 28–29 continued until the destruction of the Second Temple in 70 C.E. At that time the Jewish community discontinued the system of sacrifices described here. The role of prayer in the nonconsecrated space of the synagogues had already been recognized as appropriate for the worship of God alongside of temple sacrifices, and synagogue prayer rapidly took on even more important status. Nonetheless, the cycle of daily, weekly, and festival observance outlined in Num. 28–29 has continued to play an important part in Jewish religious life through the centuries. It is this cycle that still provides the structure for the various components of synagogue worship, both in the daily pattern of prayers and in the annual liturgical calendar (see Baruch A. Levine, *Leviticus,* 228-235).

The structure of worship described in Num. 28–29 was of course also known by Jesus and his earliest followers. Indeed, various NT stories presume some of this background. The last supper is set in a Passover context (see Matt. 26:17-29; Mark 14:12-25; Luke 22:7-38); the coming of the Holy Spirit recorded in Acts is associated with the Feast of Weeks (Pentecost, Acts 2:1). Furthermore, a range of NT passages interprets the significance of Jesus' life and especially his death in terms of the unblemished sacrificial lamb bearing the sins of the community on the Day of Atonement (see, e.g., John 1:29, 36; Acts 8:31-35; Heb. 9:25-26; 10:10; 1 Pet. 1:18-19; and the use of lamb imagery in the book of Revelation).

CHAPTER 30

This chapter considers the validity of vows, and particularly the circumstances under which vows made by women may be declared to be invalid. After a typical introduction indicating that Moses is communicating God's command (Num. 30:1), the chapter opens with a general command concerning men's vows (v. 2). The following commands concern women in their father's house (vv. 3-5), women when jurisdiction changes to their husband (vv. 6-8), divorcees and widows (v. 9), and a wife in the husband's household (vv. 10-12). The chapter concludes with an elaboration of the duty and accountability of husbands (vv. 13-15), and a concluding summation (v. 16).

This section is titled "women's vows" in most commentaries. The legislation, however, is not directed toward women, or given for their information, despite phrasing such as "if a woman. . . ." Although the legislation would serve indirectly to inform women about the status of vows they might make, the legislation in the context of Israel's culture is directed to the males of the community, to instruct them in detail about their responsibility for the making and fulfilling of vows. This emphasis is indicated by three features of the text. The first is the general introductory law in v. 2, that men must not break their own vows. This sets the stage for viewing the rest of the chapter as an explanation of what other vows men are responsible for, namely those of daughters and wives. The second clue is the elaboration of the accountability of the husband in vv. 13-15. The concluding "he shall bear her guilt" (v. 15) makes clear the seriousness of the man's duty with regard to upholding these regulations. Third, in the concluding summation (v. 16) the term "vows" does not even appear, but rather the focus is on male and female in family structure.

Given this emphasis on male responsibility, the chapter may be viewed as having a chiastic structure:

A   Man's own vow (v. 2)
    B   Father's duty (vv. 3-5)
            C   Transitional cases: from father to
                husband (vv. 6-8)
            C′ Transitional cases: from husband
                to no male (v. 9)
    B′ Husband's duty (vv. 10-12)
A′ Special emphasis on husband's direct accountability
    for vow made by his wife (vv. 13-15.)

30:1-2   After an introductory heading, the requirement that men must keep all vows they speak is stated simply and directly.

30:3-5   If a young woman, in her father's home and therefore presumably unmarried, makes a vow, its validity is dependent upon her father's action. If he does nothing, the vow is binding; if he disapproves it, the vow does not stand. He need only hear indirectly about the vow in order for the responsibility of tacit approval or explicit disapproval to fall upon him.

30:6-8   If a woman becomes married while already under obligation of a vow she has made, the husband who subsequently hears of it and disapproves may annul that vow. Here one may imagine a theoretical complication not directly addressed by the text. What if the woman's father had known of the vow and by doing nothing had given it his tacit approval? Probably the complication is indeed theoretical, since communication between husband and father-in-law is probably presumed. The law thus is presumed to concern a vow not known to the woman's father. The language of "thoughtless utterance" appears in this chapter only in this section (vv. 6, 8) and seems to stand alongside of vows. The point is apparently to emphasize that the husband is responsible for any vows his new wife might previously have made, whether carefully considered or rashly made.

30:9   Many commentators consider this verse secondary, in part because they regard it as awkwardly placed, supposing that widowhood and divorce should be treated after the discussion of marriage. The comments introducing this chapter have suggested an alternative, viewing these cases where women do bear their own responsibility for vows as a second category of women in transition. The purpose of the verse, given the larger intention of the chapter, is to show that no male member of the community is responsible for the vows of widowed or divorced women. It may be noted that never-married women whose fathers have died are not explicitly mentioned in this legislation. The mishnaic legislation of later Judaism deals with such categories and many other refinements in tractate Nedarim.

30:10-12   Husbands are responsible for vows made by their wives. Like fathers who are responsible for their daughters' vows (vv. 3-6), husbands may respond either with tacit acceptance of a vow or by nullifying the vow once it has been heard.

30:13-15   At first glance these verses appear to be a continuation of the guidelines for husbands in vv. 10-12. However, the parallel references in vv. 5 and 12 to God's forgiveness of the woman suggest that v. 12 concludes the basic unit about the husband's role. The purpose of vv. 13-15 is to underline the importance of the husband's role (and implicitly that of the father as well). His silence as tacit approval is to be taken very seriously. If he waits too long before nullifying a vow, then he himself must bear the consequences.

30:16   The summation of the legislation focuses on the households of the husband and of the father without even mentioning the word "vow," thus reinforcing the theme of male responsibility for actions of females under their authority.

Vows in ancient Israel were especially associated with hope for divine deliverance from dangerous or difficult situations. People may also have made vows routinely over matters of need and were therefore fairly often paying off such vows. Information about the payments promised in vows is quite limited. It is clear that payment of vows often involved bringing money or a sacrificial animal to a sanctuary. It is thought that payment may also have involved sexual abstinence or fasting, but these cannot be documented directly from the biblical material. The specific subject matter for women's vows (as compared to men's) is also hard to determine, although the case of Hannah (1 Sam. 1) suggests that a vow in hopes of pregnancy might be made by a woman (cf. also Prov. 31:2).

What may have been the societal function of the regulation giving men control over vows made by women in their households? It has been suggested that men would not want women to be physically weak (through fasting) or sexually unavailable (through a vow of abstinence) without good cause. Evidence for vows of this sort is slim, however, and women making a vow in hopes of conceiving a child would hardly turn to sexual abstinence. Potential economic consequences seem a more likely context for interpreting the legislation of this chapter. Vows such as Hannah's would mean loss of a male child to the economic future of the family, or perhaps a redemption payment according to the scale of Lev. 27. A vow involving offering an animal sacrifice might likewise affect the economic status of the family. The legislation gives male family heads control over this aspect of their economic destiny. The legislation thus deals with a tension between women's place in the religious sphere and their place in the family structure; in this text the needs of family structure predominate.

As with other family legislation in Numbers (see commentary on Num. 5:11-31), Christians should not attempt a literal application of this legislation in all times and places. The family system presumed in the legislation concerning vows, wherein the male head of household (father or husband) has such absolute control over the wishes of females within the household, is not inscribed by God as part of the order of creation for all time. Rather, such absolute power of one person over others (whether in families or in governments) is an indicator of the brokenness resulting from the fall of humanity. Mutuality, respect, discussion rather than decree, and genuine consideration for the needs of all parties might be more appropriate hallmarks of a family seeking to model its life together as God intends.

CHAPTER 31

The chapter opens with a call to battle against Midian. This event occupies only the first twelve verses, however; the bulk of the chapter has to do with matters of purification and booty in the aftermath of the battle.

There is division among scholars as to whether any historical kernel lies behind this narrative, or whether it is a late creation intended for theological and/or explanatory purposes. One side of this divide points out that the total extermination of the Midianites reported here is not in harmony with later narratives. For example, Judg. 6–8 reports another battle against Midian, a battle which is historically more probable. The quantities of booty taken according to the Numbers text are unrealistic, and the account focuses much more on purification and on apportionment of booty than it does on the battle itself.

On the other side, some historians suggest that the term Midian is used with differing meanings in various narratives, sometimes as here with a narrow geographic area in mind, but sometimes with a broader territory in view. According to this analysis, peoples known as Midianites inhabited a much broader range of territory than is envisaged in this story. The subgroup mentioned here may have been totally overcome, yet others would remain. Some view a brief reference to Midianites in Josh. 13:21 as an authentic ancient fragment concerning this battle, with the Numbers narrative built upon it. While a historical kernel concerning a battle with Midianites is not impossible, it is still the case that most of the chapter is not directly concerned with the battle at all. The sections concerning permitted war captives and distribution of booty may be understood as supplementing

165

and clarifying the law of Deut. 20:14-15 (Budd, *The Book of Numbers,* 334).

31:1-12   God instructs Moses to avenge Israel against Midian. The reason underlying the need for retribution is not specified here; it is made explicit only in Num. 31:16, which points the reader back to the apostasy at Baal-peor recorded in ch. 25. In effect, 31:1 is a reprise, reiterating the command given to Moses in 25:16-18. There is also a reprise of the reference in 27:12-14 to Moses' coming death in the phrase "gathered to [his] people." As in 27:12 (see commentary), this theme seems at first glance to be out of place. In this case, the reference may draw attention to this battle as Moses' last military action.

Arrangements for the battle expedition are made. Troops are selected from each tribe. Hebrew *eleph* (NRSV "thousand") may be read to mean one thousand men from each tribe on an equal basis; or it may mean a military unit or division from each tribe. The opening of 31:5 in particular (NRSV "out of the thousands of Israel") suggests the meaning of "military units." In this case, the number of warriors per unit might be smaller. (See commentary on this terminology in ch. 1.) Accompanying the troops is the priest Phinehas, who is not identified as their leader but rather is to be responsible for the sacred vessels and the trumpets. It is appropriate that Phinehas have this assignment, rather than Eleazar, for two reasons. First, it was Phinehas whose action stopped the plague at Baal-peor (25:6-9). Second, Eleazar as high priest was expected to avoid at all costs contamination by contact with a dead body (Lev. 21:11; see also commentary on Num. 16:37 and 19:4). The need for the high priest to avoid contact with a dead body makes it unlikely that he would be sent into battle. The exact religious equipment taken by Phinehas cannot be determined. The trumpets are those that were made just before the departure from the Sinai wilderness (10:2-10).

In the battle all adult males of the enemy are exterminated; among them are specified five Midianite kings and Balaam (cf. chs. 22–24; Josh. 13:21-22 mentions this battle, naming Balaam and the same five kings as those put to death). All the women and children are taken captive rather than killed (Num. 31:9);

booty is taken as the dwelling areas of the Midianites are burned. The troops return to the camp.

Certainly this act of mass extermination and scorched earth should be abhorrent to Christians today, even to those who advocate a just war theory of the necessity for violence in international relations. Given the many calls for peace among nations in the prophets' vision of the future (e.g., Isa. 2:2-4), it seems possible that this tradition and others like it may have mistakenly attributed to God Israel's own human desire for revenge or security. Even if one believes that the warfare described here did represent God's will for Israel, this story still cannot serve as a warrant for pogroms or "ethnic cleansing" today. The testimony of the Bible as a whole is clear: we are called to be peacemakers.

31:13-20   Moses, Eleazar, and other leaders meet the returning warriors outside the camp, just in time to prevent them from entering and contaminating the camp. This unit is the first of three paragraphs of command concerning purification and proper disposal of booty (Num. 31:13-20, 21-24, and 25-30).

Moses first objects to the military leaders' criteria for taking captives. Reminding them that it was the women of Midian who were responsible for the apostasy at Baal-peor (ch. 25), he commands that only the virgin females be kept alive; male children and women who have had sexual relations are to be killed. In its context, this requirement functions to insure, from a patrilineal point of view, that Midian as a people does not survive (as there are no males left alive). The requirement also insures that any women who may have been involved in the sexual relations of the apostasy do not survive. In a larger perspective, this ruling probably serves a further purpose: it sets a precedent narrowing the permissibility of war captives from that allowed in Deut. 20:14. Presumably the virgin women exempted from extermination will become sexual partners of Israelite men. An effort to regulate the treatment of female war captives is recorded in Deut. 21:10-14.

The presumption that Balaam was the instigator of the apostasy at Baal-peor (Num. 31:16) is not attested in ch. 25. The tradition of his involvement seems to suppose that since he did not succeed in cursing Israel (chs. 22–24) he must have sought another way to get Israel into trouble. The passing references to Midianite leaders alongside the Moabites in ch. 22, together with mention of both Moabites and Midianites in ch. 25, probably lent themselves to the development of this negative tradition about Balaam.

Moses also requires that proper purification from corpse contamination be carried out by the warriors and their captives, according to the regulations recorded in ch. 19. In this case there is the additional regulation that the warriors must remain outside the camp; in ch. 19 the ritual for preparing the ashes takes place outside the camp, but those contaminated are not required to move outside during their seven days of purification.

31:21-24 Eleazar gives further instructions concerning purification of various materials, attributing these commands to God through Moses. Fire is to be used for all materials where that is possible, and washing for all other materials. In addition, the water for purification (i.e., the water ritually prepared according to the instructions in ch. 19) is to be sprinkled on everything. The text does not record the fulfilment of any of the commands in 31:13-24, neither the command to kill captives nor the commands concerning purification.

31:25-47 God instructs Moses and Eleazar concerning the distribution of the live war booty, and they carry out the command. The total numbers of animals and virgin women listed are quite fantastic, even in proportion to an army of 12,000 warriors (more than 800,000 animals and 32,000 virgin women are listed in vv. 32-35). The booty is first divided into equal portions, one portion allocated to the warriors themselves and the other to the rest of the Israelites. Of the warriors' portion, one in every five hundred of each subcategory (virgin women, various kinds of animals) is given to Eleazar as "tribute," as an "offering to the LORD" (v. 29). Of the portion for the general community, one in every fifty is given to the Levites. The underlying assumption is that the priests and Levites, not being part of the twelve-tribe structure, should receive a share in the booty. Yet Eleazar's share is not technically designated for him or for the priests, but for the LORD. What Eleazar is to do with this offering for the LORD, including the thirty-two women, is not specified.

31:48-54 The military leaders report that not one Israelite is missing from those who went out to battle. This announcement that not one has died reinforces both a more immediate and a larger theological theme of the book. First, Phinehas' act (ch. 25) that stopped the plague finally and completely ended the judgment on the Israelites for their act of apostasy at Baal-peor. The retribution on the Midianites did not involve any further loss of Israelite life. Second, the theme of the second generation is lifted up. All of the second generation who were counted in the census of ch. 26 will enter the land; none is lost in this last battle beyond the Jordan.

The officers bring all the gold of their booty as an atonement offering. This presentation rounds out the sections on booty. Earlier in the chapter, instructions for purification of such objects were given, but the section on dedication of booty concerned only people and animals. The gold as listed weighed just under 200 kg., again a fantastic amount, whether from the officers only or from them on behalf of all the troops (the meaning of 31:53 is unclear). The reason for an atonement offering is not stated. It seems unlikely that thanksgiving for preservation of life would be called an "atonement" or ransom offering. Some have tied this ransom to that required in connection with a census (Exod. 30:12; Milgrom, *Numbers,* 264), but the connection between Num. 31:50 and the census of ch. 26 is not apparent. Although the law nowhere requires expiation for killing in a battle context, such an interpretation seems the most probable.

CHAPTER 32

This chapter provides an account of how the land east of the Jordan came to be settled by the tribes of Reuben, Gad, and half of Manasseh. Since this land for the most part had already been captured by the Israelites (21:21-35), it is appropriate that Moses be responsible for its distribution.

32:1-5 The Reubenites and Gadites are pictured as herders rather than as farmers. They propose to Moses, Eleazar, and the leaders of the congregation that the good pastureland east of the Jordan be given to them. Although all these leaders hear the request of the Reubenites and Gadites, the further discussion and decision involves Moses alone (32:6-27). The difficulty with the proposal of the two tribes lies in the concluding line of their request: "do not make us cross the Jordan" (v. 5b).

32:6-15 Moses interprets the plea of the Reubenites and Gadites not to cross the Jordan as potentially equivalent to the people's great rebellion against God when the spies brought their report of the land (chs. 13–14). Moses reviews that story in some detail, including the judgment on the original generation. The tribes now standing before him are addressed as a "brood of sinners" who have "risen in place of" the old generation and are risking bringing God's anger upon the people again. Underlying this assessment is the assumption that the tribes must act as a unit in entering and taking the land.

This important speech and the response to it provide a critical illustration of the difference between the generation that left Egypt and the generation poised to enter the land (Olson, *The*

Death of the Old, 141-42). Once the judgment upon the first generation is announced (ch. 14) and completed (as evidenced by the census in ch. 26), the question of the fate of the new generation still hangs in the balance. This story shows the real risk of a disastrous repetition of the earlier tragedy of disobedience, while pointing to an alternative possibility.

32:16-27   The Reubenites and Gadites propose to settle their flocks and their women and children in the Transjordanian territory they have requested. Their men will then proceed across the Jordan with the other tribes to participate in the military action until all tribes have received their land (32:16-19). Moses agrees to this arrangement, but exhorts the Reubenites and Gadites to keep to their commitment (vv. 20-24); the two tribes reiterate their preparedness "to do battle for the LORD" (vv. 25-27). Clearly sin will be averted if and when all the tribes enter the land together. The second generation, on the verge of disobedience, has drawn back from the brink; but the outcome will not be known until the time for the promise of the Reubenites and Gadites to be fulfilled.

Moses' approval of the proposal of the Reubenites and Gadites testifies yet again to the androcentric perspective of the narrative. Only the men must cross the Jordan, while wives and children may remain on the eastern side of the river. Perfect obedience in entering the land can be satisfied by full male participation, just as the census counts of the first and second generation are of adult males able to go to war.

32:28-32   Moses' decision must be announced not only to the Reubenites and Gadites, but also to those leaders who (unlike Moses) will participate in the crossing of the Jordan. The wording of Moses' declaration reveals that the Transjordanian territory is now only tentatively assigned to the two tribes. They must fulfill their obligation to cross the Jordan with the other tribes; only then will the new generation of leaders give them the land (v. 29). Again, the two tribes announce their concurrence with the agreement. This section provides a fitting conclusion to a narrative in which a potential threat to all Israel is recognized and for the time being averted. The eventual fulfilment of the commitment of these tribes, and Joshua's confirmation of their land holding, is reported in Josh. 22:1-6. The story offers an important witness of hope and of caution to future generations. God's intention to show favor to this people remains firm, but they must live obediently, guarding against taking that favor for granted.

32:33-42 The final section of the chapter specifies the land that is received by the Transjordanian tribes. Yet these verses stand in various kinds of tension with what has preceded. First, Moses is said in Num. 32:33 to "give" the land. According to the previous paragraph, this land will not be given until later. This tension may not be as severe as it appears, however, since the significant term "possession," indicating the permanence of the holding (cf. vv. 5, 29), does not appear here (Milgrom, *Numbers,* 274). Second, since Moses gives the land, the principle of awarding territory by lot announced by God (26:55) is not invoked for the territory east of the Jordan (see commentary on 34:13-15). Third, the half-tribe of Manasseh suddenly appears as an additional recipient of land in Transjordan. Fourth, the Manassites are represented as having to capture previously unconquered territory. For all these reasons, 32:33-42 are at best loosely tied to the preceding story.

Only a few of the place names mentioned in these verses can be identified with certainty. Traditions in many other parts of the OT, however, attest to Reuben, Gad, and half of Manasseh as tribes living east of the Jordan. This is shown on maps in standard biblical atlases.

CHAPTER 33

The bulk of the chapter presents a list of the stopping points of the Israelites in their wilderness journey. This list is followed by instruction for taking and distributing the land of Canaan (33:50-56). These instructions form an appropriate preface to the description of the boundaries of the Promised Land presented in ch. 34.

The itinerary consists of forty stations between the starting point of Rameses and the final location in the plains of Moab. The listing of numerous stations after the death of Aaron in the fortieth year suggests that the list of forty stations is to be thought of as a round number (like the forty years in the wilderness). These stations are not at all correlated to a year-by-year account of the wilderness journey.

The itinerary list presents many difficulties. Many of the sites listed are not mentioned in the preceding stories of the wilderness journey; some sixteen of those not mentioned are also not referred to anywhere else in the Bible. On the other hand, a good number of places that have been mentioned in the preceding wilderness stories of Exodus-Numbers are not included in the list of ch. 33. The pattern of place names that are and are not mentioned in the earlier stories does not conform consistently to any proposal for classic source division of J and P. The location of the great majority of the places listed cannot be identified at all, and there is dispute about most of those that can be tentatively identified. Even the location of Mt. Sinai is not certain.

Given these difficulties, it is no surprise to find little consensus on the origin of the list, its relationship to the preceding narratives, and its incorporation into the book of Numbers. Some suggest that the list was compiled as an extract from the preceding place names. This view seems relatively unlikely, since many previously mentioned names are omitted and a large number of names is added. It seems more probable that several lists of place names already existed. It also seems likely that these were fixed lists of sites or way stations in the geographic region of the Sinai Peninsula and lower Transjordan. Such lists were probably compiled as an aid to commercial travel in a desolate area; the lists were not intended originally for the purpose to which they are put in the biblical context. It is possible that some of the wilderness stories in Exodus and Numbers were not originally attached to place names, and that their place designations were added after an independent list was incorporated into the narrative (cf. Graham I. Davies, *The Way of the Wilderness,* 58-60).

33:1-4   The introduction to the sequence of place names reviews the historical and theological circumstances of Israel's departure from Egypt. The Egyptians had been defeated; it was the LORD who had accomplished that victory, even over the gods of Egypt.

33:5-40   A sequence of places covers the forty years in the wilderness (v. 38), concluding with mention of the death of Aaron and of the immediately following story of the king of Arad (20:22–21:3). The date of Aaron's death is given only here. Dophkah, Alush (33:12-13), and the sites designated Rithmah (v. 18b) through Hashmonah (v. 29) are not otherwise attested, nor is Abronah (v. 34).

33:41-49   Of the remaining stations, Zalmonah (v. 41) is not otherwise known in the biblical record. The itinerary concludes with the arrival in the plains of Moab (cf. 22:1).

33:50-56   This paragraph sets the stage for the remainder of Numbers, which focuses on territorial borders and on land distribution west of the Jordan. Through Moses God instructs the people on the necessity of driving out all the people living in the land west of the Jordan and of destroying all their cult images and all their places of worship. Once this is accomplished, the Israelites may settle the land given by God and divide it among the tribes by lot (cf. 26:52-56). Severe warning is given concerning the danger of not following the command to drive out the Canaanites. Not only will the Canaanites create trouble (33:55), God will destroy Israel for such disobedience (v. 56).

This insistence upon driving out (or destroying) the inhabitants of the land and destroying their sanctuaries and sacred paraphernalia is not an isolated exception. The same theme reappears, for example, in Deut. 7:2-6; Josh. 10:40-43; and Judg. 2:1-5. The violence of the exclusivist message of this text is difficult to reconcile with Christian teaching, even though similar exclusionary ideas have undergirded the Crusades and other Christian pogroms against non-Christians through the centuries. However much one may criticize the extreme measures here represented as divine will, the text is realistic about the difficulties encountered wherever different religious and ethnic groups attempt to live side by side. In the postexilic era and beyond, Judaism has generally dealt with those difficulties by trying to remain a separate community. Christianity for its part has tried to combine separatism and conversion. Comprehending the true requirements of faithfulness to one's own religious heritage in a pluralistic context is a problem as old as the era of Moses and Joshua.

CHAPTER 34

The chapter introduces the boundaries of "the land of Canaan." The boundaries described do not include the region of central and southern Transjordan that has been assigned to Reuben, Gad, and half of Manasseh in Num. 32. God also appoints tribal leaders who will assist with the apportioning of the land.

34:1-12   The boundary description begins with the southerly side, running from the lower end of the Dead Sea westward, passing south of Kadesh to the Wadi (Brook) of Egypt and thence to the Mediterranean Sea. The west boundary is the Great (i.e., Mediterranean) Sea. On the north side, the boundary description moves eastward from the Mediterranean to a point beyond Lebo-hamath. (The Mt. Hor mentioned in 34:7 must be located in the north, and thus is not the same mountain where Aaron died.) The eastern boundary is marked southward from the far point of the northern side; it includes the eastern slopes of the Sea of Chinnereth (Galilee or Gennesaret). At the southern end of the Sea of Chinnereth the line meets the Jordan River and follows the river down to the Dead Sea, thus completing the description at its starting point.

Although some of the boundary points listed cannot be identified, historical geographers can do much more with this list than with the itinerary list of ch. 33. The overall boundaries described in ch. 34 can be reasonably closely drawn on a map. However, the historical basis of this boundary description is less certain. It has many similarities to the boundary description found in Josh. 15:1-4, as well as to lists in Ezek. 47:15-20 and 48:1. The extent of the boundaries given is greater than the traditional expression

176

"from Dan to Beer-sheba" (e.g., Judg. 20:1); rather, the boundaries move from "Lebo-hamath to the Wadi of Egypt" (1 Kgs. 8:65; Budd, *The Book of Numbers,* 365). In the period of Israel's occupation of Canaan, the boundaries described seem to fit best with the era of David and Solomon, although the Philistine coastal area included here was never really controlled by Israel. Possibly the exilic or postexilic compiler of this list was using boundary lists like those known from Joshua and Ezekiel to describe the territory of the United Monarchy.

It should also be noted that the boundaries described have been argued to match precisely the boundaries of part of the Egyptian New Kingdom empire known as the province of Canaan in the thirteenth century B.C.E. (Roland de Vaux, "Le pays de Canaan"). A persistent memory of this ancient definition of the region called Canaan may explain in part why the boundary described in this tradition does not include Israel's actual holdings in Transjordan.

34:13-15 The land just described is to be apportioned by lot to the nine and one-half tribes who have not received land in Transjordan. These verses remind the reader that Reuben, Gad, and half of Manasseh have already been assigned territory, and that their territory is not included within the preceding boundaries. Jacob Milgrom (*Numbers,* 502) points out that Numbers makes no mention of a divine command to capture the central and southern Transjordanian territory (Num. 21:21-35; contrast Deut. 2:24) and also that no mention is made of the use of lots when Moses assigned that territory to the two and one-half tribes (Num. 32:33). Relating these two observations to the omission of this same territory from the boundary list of 34:1-14, Milgrom suggests that the tradition of Numbers did not regard the Transjordanian territory as part of the Promised Land. According to Numbers only the land to be taken after crossing the Jordan was understood to be given by God.

34:16-29 God gives Moses a list of those tribal leaders who are to assist Eleazar and Joshua when it is time to apportion the land. Ten names are given, one from each of the nine and one-half tribes who will possess portions of the land of Canaan demarcated in vv. 1-12. The giving of such a list is reminiscent of the list of leaders called upon to assist in the initial census in ch. 1. Moses cannot enter the land himself, and thus he cannot direct the apportionment. But all the preparations are made through Moses, just as the Chronicler presents David as responsible for all details of the Jerusalem temple except for its actual construction (Budd, *The Book of Numbers*, 368).

CHAPTER 35

The chapter continues the theme of land distribution introduced in ch. 34. Here special arrangements are introduced for the Levites who will not receive a regular land apportionment like that of the other Israelites. Related to these provisions for the Levites are provisions for cities of refuge for use by a person who has caused the death of another.

35:1-8 God commands that forty-eight towns with surrounding pasturelands shall be given over to the Levites as space for living and for grazing their herds and flocks. The towns are to be selected from among all the tribal territories, with the amount of land ceded to the Levites by each tribe being proportional to the size of its territorial allotment (35:8).

The question of where the Levites should live arises quite logically from the preceding material in Numbers. The Levites have not been counted among the twelve tribes but have been reckoned separately in the census reports of the opening chapters (1:49; 3:15) and again in the second census of ch. 26. It is even stated in 26:62 that the Levites were numbered separately "because there was no allotment given to them among the Israelites." Considering the Levites' duties, however, the scattering of the Levites among the twelve tribal areas is surprising. It seems to stand in tension with the responsibilities of the Levites for care of the tabernacle and its equipment as described in chs. 3–4. The book of Numbers ends without any further reference to the wilderness tabernacle. Also, 18:24 suggests that the Levites do not need any land because they are receiving financial support through the tithes of the Israelites.

179

Texts about the Levites' land and/or support found elsewhere in the OT compound rather than resolve these tensions. Ezekiel 48:13-14 gives a single territory to the Levites, rather than scattered towns, although all the tribal territories are idealized in this chapter. The most closely related text, Josh. 21, lists towns given to various Levitical groups and is clearly intended as the fulfilment of the command of Num. 35. Historical geographers point out, however, that the towns named in Josh. 21 are not proportionately dispersed. The distribution among tribes is nearly equal, not proportional either to their varying populations or to the size of their territorial holdings. Also, some towns listed are so close together that the surrounding grazing territories would overlap. Scholars who believe that there were actually Levitical towns have argued over the dating of this list of cities in Joshua; some have placed it as early as the tenth century while other have proposed a date as late as the seventh century B.C.E. Others regard the Levitical towns as postexilic arrangement, while still others think these verses present an idealized situation that never actually existed. The main lines of scholarly debate are conveniently summarized in Budd, *The Book of Numbers,* 370-76. The status of the town list and the entire conception of Levitical towns can only be evaluated in light of the much disputed history of Israel's priesthood and the relation of the Levites to the priests (see Introduction).

Whatever one concludes about the implementation of the command concerning the towns, the goal of having all territorial arrangements announced by God through Moses is clear. Somewhere in the later history of the group known as Levites, some question of territory or geographic distribution must have arisen. As with the question of inheritance by daughters with no brothers (Num. 27 and 36), the decision is attributed to the wilderness period.

The measuring system for the space allotted for pasturage assumes a central point from which one measures 1,000 cubits (about 450 m.) toward each compass point. The borders are then created as a square of 2,000 cubits per side. However, the 1,000-cubit measurements are actually taken from the outsides of the town wall on each side. This means that the resultant square or rectangle is a bit larger than 2,000 cubits per side, but insures that town expansion does not erase adequate pasturage. The rabbinic tradition of the distance an observant Jew may walk on the sabbath is based on the pasturage space as calculated in 35:4-5 (Jacob Milgrom, "The Levitic Town").

35:9-15 The instruction for establishing cities of refuge follows upon the mention in v. 6 that six of these shall be included among the Levitical towns. There are to be three such cities on each side of the Jordan. They may be used by any Israelite, resident alien, or transient alien who kills a person without intent. The law presumes that a relative of the dead person will seek to avenge the death by killing the slayer. Upon reaching a city of refuge, the slayer must be protected until a trial that will determine whether the killing was intentional or not. The custom of places of asylum for slayers and the duty of a blood relative to avenge a person killed are known from various cultures around the world. This legislation and the rationale for it are also set forth in Deut. 19:1-13.

Reference to a trial makes clear that anyone who kills another and claims "without intent" may flee to a city of refuge (Num. 35:11-12). As can be seen in the remainder of the chapter, however, the cities of refuge also become the actual dwelling place of those judged to be unintentional killers (vv. 25, 28). Hence the instruction regarding these cities focuses upon them as places for those who kill without intent. The fulfilment of this command to designate six cities, together with a summary of the procedure in such cases, is reported in Josh. 20.

35:16-21 A series of examples of methods and circumstances of killing describes the conditions of murder, as opposed to killing without intent. Death caused by using a potentially lethal weapon is classified as murder. So is death that results from action out of hatred or premeditation (lying in wait) even if no weapon is used. In such cases, the death may be avenged by putting the killer to death.

35:22-29 Numbers 35:22-23 illustrate the alternative possi-

181

bilities, in which the death occurs without intent. The examples of v. 22 seem to refer to fights without weapons or unpremeditated acts of sudden anger not intended to cause death, although death did occur. The examples in v. 23 represent the category of accidents. The series of case illustrations from v. 16 through v. 23 thus begins with the most obvious cases of deliberate murder (use of lethal weapon) and ends with the most obvious cases of accidental killing. In the middle are more ambiguous cases where questions of intent and premeditation are less obvious; some of these are judged to be murder, others unintentional killing. A long tradition of law and case precedents in Western societies seeks to follow through on these categories in assessing guilt or innocence and in establishing a range of penalties graded according to these circumstances.

Verses 24-29 set forth the proper response in cases of slaying without intent. The "congregation" (the community constituted for sacral responsibility) is called upon to judge whether or not the death is without intent. If the congregation judges in favor of the slayer, the congregation shall then see to it that the slayer is not put to death but is conveyed safely to the city of refuge (v. 25). Thus it appears that the congregation involved in the trial is not the people of the city of refuge itself, as might be thought from v. 12. Rather, the trial is conducted by the community that knows the persons and the circumstances of the case. Although the killing occurred without intent, indeed even if it was completely accidental, the person who caused that death must pay a penalty for the shedding of blood by remaining in the city of refuge "until the death of the high priest." Such an indeterminate sentence is far removed from those of many modern cultures that focus on numbers of years, months, and days.

Together with the term "congregation" and the references to pollution in vv. 33-34, the reference to the death of the high priest reinforces the perspective that this legislation belongs to the sphere of what is sacred. It is true that the dead person has been wronged, and also the family of the person (as represented by the avenger's claim). But more than that, the holy community becomes polluted and its proper relationship to God disrupted by such an untimely death, whether deliberate or without intent.

The legislation concerning the use of these cities of refuge does not specify whether this regulation applied to men only or to women as well as men. It is probable that in ancient Israel, as in most contemporary cultures, women caused a very small percentage of the deaths considered under this law. Thus the androcentric circles that codified and preserved this legislation may not have thought about the situation of women. In theory, both women and men are included under any biblical law that does not specify one sex; yet based on our general knowledge of the role of women in Israelite culture, it seems unlikely that a woman who killed someone could live alone in a strange city for an indefinite period.

35:30-34   The chapter concludes with a further protection of the accused and additional regulations placing the taking of human life into the sacral sphere. To protect the accused, a verdict requiring the death penalty must be based on testimony of more than one witness. Although the text is not explicit, this is presumed to mean that at least two witnesses must agree that the case was murder, not unintentional death (cf. Deut. 17:6, where the rule is extended to another capital offense, and Deut. 19:15, where the rule apparently applies to any kind of conviction, not just to the death penalty).

No financial payment is permitted as a substitute for the prescribed death penalty for a convicted murderer (Num. 35:31). Nor is payment permitted to reduce the time that the unintentional killer must spend in a city of refuge (v. 32). The theological reason for the prohibition of ransom is expressed in vv. 33-34: in the shedding of blood the land becomes polluted, and no expiation is permitted except by blood. The death of the murderer provides expiation for the death of the victim of deliberate homicide. The eventual death of the high priest becomes in effect the expiation for the death of the victim of an unintentional killing. Its effectiveness, however, is dependent upon the slayer remaining in the city of refuge.

By contrast to most modern debates about capital punishment, the strictness of these requirements is not associated with preventing further crimes. There is no mention of deterrence or of financial considerations of the expense of incarceration. The primary concern is not even with avenging the innocent. Rather, these regulations are grounded solely in Israel's understanding of God's presence dwelling in the midst of the people (v. 34). A holy God cannot be present in the midst of an unholy people; the community must therefore take proper steps to undo the pollution caused by shedding of blood. In the cases of natural death (ch. 19) or contact with dead bodies in battle (ch. 31), rites of purification are specified. In cases of intentional or unintentional homicide, however, expiation without substitution is required.

CHAPTER 36

The book of Numbers concludes with a return to the story of the daughters of Zelophehad (cf. ch. 27). This story forms an appropriate conclusion to the book in at least three respects. First, the two parts of this story, 27:1-11 and 36:1-13, form a bracket holding together all the loosely connected material presented after the second census of ch. 26.

Second, as has been indicated in the commentary, nearly all of the material of chs. 27–36 is directed in some way toward life in the land and the concerns of the new generation to whom God will give possession of the land. The theme of proper inheritance, central to land distribution, is introduced in ch. 26 and appears several times in these chapters. Here the themes of inheritance and distribution are brought together in explicit connection. The topic is particularly appropriate for Moses' last legislative instruction.

Third, the theme of the lack of sin in the wilderness life of the second generation is established by the conclusion of the story, 36:10-12. This theme is implicitly present after the census of ch. 26 in the absence of any further murmuring narratives. It is suggested more strongly by the story of the Reubenites and Gadites in ch. 32. Their obedience, however, will not be fully tested until the crossing of the Jordan. Here the ending of Numbers specifies the daughters' full obedience to Moses' commands. Through this concluding narrative the contrast between the first and second generation is finally and firmly established.

36:1-4 The male relatives of Zelophehad's tribe have recognized a serious problem (from their point of view) in the inheritance ruling promulgated by Moses concerning Zelophehad's daughters. They present their claim to Moses, the leaders, and the heads of the ancestral houses. Comparison to 27:2 shows that the setting for the challenge has changed. There Eleazar and the tent of meeting are mentioned; here the appeal and decision are not set in a sacral context.

The substance of the men's complaint appears in 36:3. If the women who have inherited land under the law of ch. 27 marry outside their own tribe, the land they hold will be transferred to that tribe. The holdings of the Manassite tribe to which Zelophehad belonged will be reduced. The men argue that not even the law of jubilee, which provides for redistribution of land to its original owners, will be able to overcome this change of land distribution. Rather, it will function to make it even more permanent (36:4).

Here the theme of the father's name (27:4) has disappeared and the focus has shifted to male property rights. The presupposition of the narrative is that the women's land holding was only temporary, until their marriage; the question is which males have the right to acquire the property. Ancient Israel was a subsistence level agrarian society. Since land potentially suitable for farming or herding would come into the husband's family on a permanent basis, men presumably would seek out land-holding women for marriage.

36:5-9   Moses announces divine concurrence with the concern of the petition, first addressing the specific case (36:6-7) and then promulgating a general rule (vv. 8-9). Again the narrative pattern differs in details from ch. 27. There Moses consulted God and the answer was given in terms of a command placed in the mouth of God and addressed to Moses (27:5-11); in ch. 27 Moses' actual report to the people is not recorded. Here, by contrast, the speech of response is entirely in the mouth of Moses to the Israelites; the commands are attributed to God, but there is no explicit report that Moses brought the case before God (contrast 27:5).

The ruling is that the daughters may marry "whom they think best," with the limitation that they are required to marry someone within "a clan of their father's tribe" (36:6). The rationale is that the land must stay in the possession of the tribe to which it is originally allotted; land must not be transferred around among the tribes.

The phrase "whom they think best" may suggest that these women whose fathers had died were free to select their own husbands. Knowledge of marriage customs in ancient Israel is limited, but most scholars believe that families played an important role in arranging marriages. If land-holding women (i.e., women without fathers or brothers) were able to make their own choice of husband, the legislation here would serve to limit their range of options. If, on the other hand, the choice of a husband for such a woman lay even partially in control of other male relatives, this legislation would help to control squabbles that might break out among the men about what arrangement to make.

In this passage, the socioeconomic problem of access to arable land is intertwined with the theological interpretation of God's intention concerning tribal allotments. This intertwining is seen especially in the uses of the terms "clan" and "tribe." The language of the male relatives' complaint and the language of the rationale for the decision both focus on the religious category of the "tribe." The decision itself (vv. 6, 8) and the fulfilment of the command by the daughters (vv. 10-12) focus on the narrower socioeconomic category of "clan." If the real purpose of the legislation were to prevent land changing hands at the tribal level, the women could have been given a much wider choice of possible husbands. Thus it is likely that this law was intended to control property shifting in quite localized settings. The attached rationale is a loosely connected theological explanation based on a tradition of inalienable divine allotments to the various tribes.

36:10-12   The obedience of the five women to Moses' command is reported. They marry within a clan of the Manassites, and the land remains where it theologically and socioeconomically belongs, "in the tribe of their father's clan." As indicated in the comments above, the obedience of the daughters forms a highly appropriate theological conclusion to the book of Numbers.

From the narrator's viewpoint, the daughters of Zelophehad, obedient to God, lived happily ever after. This verdict, however, calls for careful theological reflection, even as does the instruction to drive out the Canaanites (33:50-56; see commentary). The daughters of Zelophehad, and other women like them, were granted a fresh option through land holding; yet restrictions were soon imposed. The decisions, presented as coming from God, functioned to support male interests in an androcentric society. Throughout the centuries, Christians have reflected in various ways upon the relationship between their understanding of the gospel and their view of the roles of men and women in their own cultures. This concluding story of the book of Numbers, with its clear use of religious warrants to support cultural presuppositions, should prompt continuing consideration of the relationship between faith and culture in every context.

36:13 The final verse of Numbers looks back upon the concluding section of the book. The arrival of the people in the "plains of Moab" is reported at the beginning of the Balaam story (22:1). The reference to "commandments and ordinances," however, calls attention particularly to the section of Numbers after the second census (ch. 26), in which the legislative material is embedded. The generational structure of the book is implicitly confirmed.

The mention of the plains of Moab not only looks backward, however. It also provides a transition forward to Moses' speeches in Deuteronomy, which are given in the plains of Moab. From the plains of Moab, Moses ascends Mt. Nebo to view the Promised Land before his death (Deut. 34:1; cf. Num. 27:12-14). Moses is mourned in the plains of Moab (Deut. 34:8). The final words of Numbers, "by the Jordan at Jericho," set the reader's sights even further ahead, to the crossing of the Jordan River to Jericho. Reported in the opening chapters of the book of Joshua, this sacred moment of crossing into the land and the taking of Jericho will inaugurate the next era in the life of God's people — an era in the Promised Land, under the leadership of Joshua (cf. Num. 27:16-23) as successor to Moses.

SELECTED BIBLIOGRAPHY

Commentaries

Ashley, Timothy R. *The Book of Numbers.* New International Commentary on the Old Testament (Grand Rapids: Wm. B. Eerdmans, 1993).

> *A recent translation and technical commentary. Makes use of current linguistic and text-critical resources.*

Budd, Philip J. *The Book of Numbers.* Word Biblical Commentary 5 (Waco: Word, 1984).

> *Gives attention to history of scholarship on individual texts, with special attention to form and redaction criticism, plus extensive bibliography.*

Gray, George Buchanan. *A Critical and Exegetical Commentary on Numbers.* International Critical Commentary (New York: Scribner's and Edinburgh: T. & T. Clark, 1903).

> *A classic exposition in the source-critical tradition of scholarship.*

Levine, Baruch A. *Leviticus.* Jewish Publication Society Torah Commentary (New York: Jewish Publication Society, 1989).

> *Assesses the actual practice and significance of Israel's ritual legislation by giving attention both to the ancient Near Eastern context and to interpretation in the subsequent Jewish community.*

―――. *Numbers 1–20.* Anchor Bible 4 (New York: Doubleday, 1993).

> *Fresh translation with extensive use of Near Eastern backgrounds. Special attention to ritual materials.*

Mays, James Luther. *The Book of Leviticus–The Book of Numbers.* Layman's Commentary (Richmond: John Knox, 1963).

> *A nontechnical treatment emphasizing the place of Numbers in the larger pentateuchal context.*

Milgrom, Jacob. *Leviticus 1–16*. Anchor Bible 3 (New York: Doubleday, 1991).

    A monumental study of Israel's sacrificial, cultic, and impurity legislation.

————. *Numbers*. Jewish Publications Society Torah Commentary (New York: Jewish Publication Society, 1990).

    Focuses on final form of the text with special attention to rabbinic interpretation. Extensive notes on individual words.

Noth, Martin. *Numbers*. Old Testament Library (Philadephia: Westminster and London: SCM, 1968).

    Focuses on the growth of the tradition in its oral and written stages.

de Vaulx, Jules. *Les Nombres*. Sources bibliques (Paris: J. Gabalda, 1972).

    Balances traditio-historical and theological interpretation.

Other Books

Boling, Robert G. *The Early Biblical Community in Transjordan* (Sheffield: Almond, 1988).

Brueggemann, Walter. *The Land: Place as Gift, Promise, and Challenge in Biblical Faith*. Overtures to Biblical Theology (Philadelphia: Fortress, 1977).

    A theological survey of the theme of land in Hebrew scripture.

Buber, Martin. *Moses: The Revelation and the Covenant* (Oxford: East and West Library, 1946; repr. Atlantic Highlands, N.J.: Humanities Press International, 1988).

    An attempt to study the person and historical contribution of Moses.

Burns, Rita J. *Has the Lord Indeed Spoken Only through Moses? A Study of the Biblical Portrait of Miriam*. SBL Dissertation 84 (Atlanta: Scholars' Press, 1987).

Cody, Aelred. *A History of Old Testament Priesthood*. Analecta Biblica 35 (Rome: Pontifical Biblical Institute, 1969).

    Argues for a late fictional connection of the Zadokites to Aaron.

Cross, Frank Moore, Jr. *Canaanite Myth and Hebrew Epic: Essays in the History of the Religion of Israel* (Cambridge, Mass.: Harvard University Press, 1973).

    Proposes that two priestly families, one descended from Aaron and one from Moses, were in competition at the beginning of the Monarchy.

Davies, Graham I. *The Way of the Wilderness: A Geographical Study of the Wilderness Itineraries in the Old Testament.* Society for Old Testament Study Monograph 5 (Cambridge: Cambridge University Press, 1979).

> *Uses Jewish, Christian, and Arabic sources, together with basic principles of toponymy, to identify sites and routes in the Sinai Peninsula and Transjordan.*

Douglas, Mary. *In the Wilderness: The Doctrine of Defilement in the Book of Numbers.* Journal for the Study of the Old Testament Supplement 158 (Sheffield: JSOT Press, 1993).

> *Approaching Numbers as an anthropologist, Douglas finds an anti-exclusionary theme supporting openness toward Samaritans in the postexilic period. She also proposes a literary structure based on alternating strands of narrative and law, with chiastic patterns in each category of material.*

————. *Purity and Danger* (London: Routledge and Kegan Paul, 1966, and New York: Praeger, 1970).

> *An anthropological analysis of Israel's purity codes, with special attention to clean and unclean animals.*

Felder, Cain Hope. *Troubling Biblical Waters: Race, Class, and Family* (Maryknoll, N.Y.: Orbis, 1989).

> *A discussion of various issues concerning the relationship of the Bible to ancient Africa and to contemporary African-American concerns. See especially the discussion of Moses' wife, 139ff.*

Fritz, Volkmar. *Israel in der Wüste: Traditionsgeschichtliche Untersuchung der Wüstenüberlieferung des Jahwisten.* Marburger theologische Studien 7 (Marburg: N. G. Elwert, 1970).

> *Identification of texts from the Yahwistic (J) source, along with a traditio-historical study of them, with a review of results and implications for geography, history, and theology.*

Gammie, John G. *Holiness in Israel* (Minneapolis: Fortress, 1989).

> *Describes perspectives on holiness in various types of OT literature.*

Gottwald, Norman Karol. *The Tribes of Yahweh: A Sociology of the Religion of Liberated Israel, 1230-1050 B.C.E.* (Maryknoll, N.Y.: Orbis, 1979).

> *A study of the emergence of Israel in Canaan, with special attention to anthropological evidence for tribal structures.*

Gressmann, Hugo. *Mose und seine Zeit: Ein Kommentar zu den Mose-Sagen.* Forschungen zur Religion und Literatur des Alten und Neuen Testaments N.S. 1 (Göttingen: Vandenhoeck & Ruprecht, 1913).

A classic form-critical treatment of many passages from Numbers.

Hackett, Jo Ann. *The Balaam Text from Deir 'Alla.* Harvard Semitic Monographs 31 (Chico: Scholars Press, 1984).

A linguistic and orthographic study of an ancient inscription referring to "Balaam Son of Beor," with discussion of earlier treatments of the inscription.

Haran, Menahem. *Temples and Temple-Service in Ancient Israel: An Inquiry into the Character of Cult Phenomena and the Historical Setting of the Priestly School* (Oxford: Clarendon, 1978).

Argues that the Priestly material of the Pentateuch reflects a utopian vision set forth during the reign of Hezekiah (ca. 715-687 B.C.E.).

Klein, Ralph W. *Israel in Exile* (Philadelphia: Fortress, 1979).

Considers theological responses to the Babylonian exile in various parts of the Hebrew scriptures, with special attention in ch. 6 to the Priestly writers.

Noth, Martin. *A History of Pentateuchal Traditions* (Englewood Cliffs, N.J.: Prentice Hall, 1972; repr. Atlanta: Scholars Press, 1989).

A rigorous application of traditio-historical methodology to the Pentateuch, with special focus on Exodus and Numbers.

Olson, Dennis T. *The Death of the Old and the Birth of the New: The Framework of the Book of Numbers and the Pentateuch.* Brown Judaic Studies 71 (Chico: Scholars' Press, 1985).

The census texts in Num. 1 and 26 are seen to provide a key to the outline of Numbers and to a theological interpretation of the book as a whole.

Plaskow, Judith. *Standing Again at Sinai: Judaism from a Feminist Perspective* (San Francisco: Harper and Row, 1990).

Seybold, Klaus. *Der aaronitische Segen: Studien zu Numeri 6,22-27* (Neukirchen-Vluyn: Neukirchener Verlag, 1977).

Discusses the use of the name of God, the possible liturgical setting of the blessing, and its overall theological meaning.

Walzer, Michael. *Exodus and Revolution* (New York: Basic Books, 1985).

Weems, Renita J. *Just a Sister Away: A Womanist Vision of Women's Relationships in the Bible* (San Diego: LuraMedia, 1988).

A series of Bible studies, with questions for thought and use in discussion. See especially "In Law, In Love: Miriam and Her Cushite Sister-in-Law," 71-84.

Wellhausen, Julius. *Prolegomena to the History of Ancient Israel*

(Cleveland: World, 1957; repr. Magnolia, Mass.: Peter Smith, 1973). [Translation of 1878 German 1st ed.]

A classic presentation of the history of Israel's religion in relationship to the themes and dates of pentateuchal sources.

Westermann, Claus. *Blessing in the Bible and the Life of the Church.* Overtures to Biblical Theology (Philadelphia: Fortress, 1978).

Considers the larger context of blessing in the Old and New Testaments and in church rituals.

Wright, George Ernest. *Biblical Archaeology* (Philadelphia: Westminster, 1957; rev. ed. 1962).

Includes archaeological evidence for the wilderness route, dating, and features of desert life.

Articles

Albright, William Foxwell. "The Oracles of Balaam," *Journal of Biblical Literature* 63 (1944): 207-233.

A technical study of orthography, poetry, and vocabulary, with comments on historical allusions.

Bailey, Randall C. "Beyond Identification: The Use of Africans in Old Testament Poetry and Narratives," in *Stony the Road We Trod: African American Biblical Interpretation,* ed. Cain Hope Felder (Minneapolis: Fortress, 1991), 165-184.

Coats, George W. "Balaam: Sinner or Saint?" *Biblical Research* 18 (1973): 21-29.

Argues that the genre of the Balaam story is legend, emphasizing the virtue of its hero, not the mighty acts of God.

Davies, Graham I. "The Wilderness Itineraries: A Comparative Study," *Tyndale Bulletin* 25 (1974): 46-81.

Frymer-Kensky, Tikva. "The Strange Case of the Suspected *Sotah* (Numbers V 11-31)," *Vetus Testamentum* 34 (1984): 11-26.

Kinukawa, Hisako. "The Story of the Hemorrhaging Woman (Mark 5:25-34) Read from a Japanese Feminist Context," *Biblical Interpretation* 2 (1994): 283-293.

Considers implications for the church of Jesus' challenge to the laws of impurity.

Lohfink, Norbert. "Die Ursünden in der priesterlichen Geschichtserzählung," in *Die Zeit Jesu.* Festschrift Heinrich Schlier, ed. Günther Bornkamm and Karl Rahner (Freiburg: Herder, 1970), 38-57.

The sin of Moses and Aaron symbolizes the sin of the religious leaders of the exilic period.

MacDonald, Burton. "Archaeology of Edom," *Anchor Bible Dictionary* (New York: Doubleday, 1992), 2:295-301.

Mendenhall, George E. "The Census Lists of Numbers 1 and 26," *Journal of Biblical Literature* 77 (1958): 52-66.
Argues that the word for "thousand" originally meant a tribal subunit.

Milgrom, Jacob. "The Levitic Town: An Exercise in Realistic Town Planning," *Journal of Jewish Studies* 33 (1982): 185-88.

Miller, Patrick D. "The Blessing of God: An Interpretation of Numbers 6:22-27," *Interpretation* 29 (1975): 240-251.
A brief treatment of theological themes in the Aaronic benediction, emphasizing the providence of God.

Rainey, Anson F. "The Order of Sacrifices in Old Testament Ritual Texts," *Biblica* 51 (1970): 485-498.

Sakenfeld, Katharine Doob, "Feminist Biblical Interpretation," *Theology Today* 46 (1989): 154-168.
Literary and historical analysis of the narratives about the daughters of Zelophehad (Num. 27, 36).

———. "The Problem of Divine Forgiveness in Numbers 14," *Catholic Biblical Quarterly* 37 (1975): 317-330.
A critical and theological analysis of the spy narrative.

———. "Theological and Redactional Problems in Numbers 20:2-13," in *Understanding the Word.* Festschrift Bernhard W. Anderson. Journal for the Study of the Old Testamant Supplement 37 (Sheffield: JSOT Press, 1985), 133-154.
An argument for balance between the roles of Moses and Aaron in the final form of the Pentateuch.

Scott, R. B. Y. "Weights and Measures of the Bible," *Biblical Archaeologist* 22 (1959): 22-40.

de Vaux, Roland. "Le pays de Canaan," *Journal of the American Oriental Society* 88 (1968): 23-30.

Wharton, James A. "The Command to Bless: An Exposition of Numbers 22:41–23:25," *Interpretation* 13 (1959): 37-48.
Emphasizes the power of God's word and the obedience of the prophet as key themes present in the Balaam narrative.